ENCYCLOPEDIA OF MAMMALS

ENCYCLOPEDIA OF MAMMALS

VOLUME 1
Aar–Bad

MARSHALL CAVENDISH

NEW YORK • LONDON • TORONTO • SYDNEY

EDITORIAL CONTRIBUTORS

Tony Hare, PhD

Mark Lambert, BSc

EDITORIAL CONSULTANT

Dan Wharton,
Director of the Central Park Wildlife Center,
Wildlife Conservation Society

EDITORIAL STAFF

Editor: Andrew Brown

Designer: Melissa Stokes

Production: Craig Chubb

The publisher is grateful for the special assistance of

Dorene Bolze, Senior Policy Analyst,
International Programs, Wildlife Conservation Society

Greg Early, Associate Curator,
New England Aquarium

Randy Fulk, Curator of Research,
North Carolina Zoological Park

Laurie Marker-Kraus, Co-Director,
Cheetah Conservation Fund

Lori Perkins, Conservation Biologist,
Zoo Atlanta

Gaza Teleki

Denis Thoney, Curator of Saltwater Fish,
Aquarium for Wildlife Conservation

Christian Wemmer, Associate Director for Conservation,
National Zoological Park Conservation and Research Center

CHAPTER-OPENER PICTURE CREDITS
Volume One: p. 2, Michael P. Price/Bruce Coleman Ltd.; p. 28, Kenneth W. Fink/Ardea; p. 54, K. & K. Amman/Planet Earth Pictures; p. 80, Jeff Foott/Survival Anglia; p. 106, Jeff Foott/Survival Anglia
Volume Two: p. 132, Kenneth W. Fink/Ardea; p. 158, Jeff Foott/Survival Anglia; p. 184, Raymond A. Mendez/Oxford Scientific Films; p. 210, Wayne Lankinen/Aquila; p. 236, Jeff Foott/Survival Anglia; p. 262, Stephen Kraseman/ZEFA
Volume Three: p. 288, Masahiro Iijima/Ardea; p. 314, Wayne Lankinen/Aquila; p. 340, Kenneth W. Fink/Ardea; p. 366, E.A. Janes/NHPA; p. 392, James Robinson/Oxford Scientific Films; p. 418, Anup Shah/Planet Earth Pictures
Volume Four: p. 444, Stan Osolinski/Oxford Scientific Films; p. 470, Tom Brakefield; p. 496, Rod Williams/Bruce Coleman Ltd.; p. 522, Cameron Read/Planet Earth Pictures; p. 548, Ardea; p. 574, Stanley Breeden/Oxford Scientific Films
Volume Five: p. 600, Jonathon Scott/Planet Earth Pictures; p. 626, Kevin Schafer/NHPA; p. 652, Clem Haagner/Ardea; p. 678, Mary Clay/Planet Earth Pictures; p. 704, Wayne Lankinen/Aquila; p. 730, Stephen Dalton/NHPA
Volume Six: p. 756, Ken Oake/Partridge Films Ltd./Oxford Scientific Films; p. 782, Terry Whittaker/Frank Lane Picture Agency; p. 808, Gerard Lacz/NHPA; p. 834, Henry Ausloos/NHPA; p. 860, Michael Leach/Oxford Scientific Films; p. 886, ZEFA
Volume Seven: p. 912, Jane Burton/Bruce Coleman Ltd.; p. 938, Frithjof Skibbe/Oxford Scientific Films; p. 964, J.F. Preedy/Aquila; p. 990, Jonathon Scott/Planet Earth Pictures; p. 1016, ANT/NHPA; p. 1042, Bob Campbell/Survival Anglia
Volume Eight: p. 1068, Gerald Cubitt/Bruce Coleman Ltd.; p. 1094, Brian Kenney/Planet Earth Pictures; p. 1120, Bruce Coleman Ltd.; p. 1146, Steve Turner/Oxford Scientific Films; p. 1172, Ardea; p. 1198, Gerard Lacz/NHPA

Volume Nine: p. 1224, Purdy & Matthews/Tony Stone Worldwide; p. 1250, Manfred Danegger/NHPA; p. 1276, Ken Lucas/Planet Earth Pictures; p. 1302, Wayne Lankinen/Aquila; p. 1328, David McDonald/Oxford Scientific Films; p. 1354, Kaj Halberg/Biofotos
Volume Ten: p. 1380, David Woodfall/NHPA; p. 1406, Gunter Ziesler/Bruce Coleman Ltd.; p. 1432, Rod Williams/Bruce Coleman Ltd.; p. 1458, Toni Angermayer/Oxford Scientific Films; p. 1484, Ken King/Planet Earth Pictures; p. 1510, David Middleton/NHPA
Volume Eleven: p. 1536, Jeff Foott/Survival Anglia; p. 1562, Guiliano Colliva/The Image Bank; p. 1588, Henry Auless/WWF International; p. 1614, Clem Haagner/Ardea; p. 1640, Jeff Foott/Survival Anglia; p. 1666, Bryan & Cherry Alexander
Volume Twelve: p. 1692, Janet Haag/Natural Science Photos; p. 1718, Roger Brown/Oxford Scientific Films; p. 1744, Jeff Foott/Survival Anglia; p. 1770, Tom McHugh/Oxford Scientific Films; p. 1796, Ian Beames/Ardea; p. 1822, Robert Maier/Aquila
Volume Thirteen: p. 1848, Rod Williams/Bruce Coleman Ltd.; p. 1874, Dr. F. Koster/Survival Anglia; p. 1900, J.O. Wirminghaus/Planet Earth Pictures; p. 1926, Ken Lucas/Planet Earth Pictures; p. 1952, Jeff Foott/Survival Anglia; p. 1978, Kevin Schafer/NHPA
Volume Fourteen: p. 2004, Steve Turner/Oxford Scientific Films; p. 2030, Rod Williams/Bruce Coleman Ltd.; p. 2056, John Lythgoe/Planet Earth Pictures; p. 2082, Gerard Lacz/NHPA; p. 2108, Jeff Foott/Survival Anglia; p. 2134, Steve Turner/Oxford Scientific Films
Volume Fifteen: p. 2160, John Garret/Tony Stone Worldwide; p. 2186, Cameron Read/Planet Earth Pictures; p. 2212, Hans Reinhard/Tony Stone Worldwide; p. 2238, Agence Nature/NHPA; p. 2264, Ken King/Planet Earth Pictures; p. 2290, Dave Watts/ANT/NHPA
Volume Sixteen: p. 2316, ANT/NHPA; p. 2342, Marc Webber/Planet Earth Pictures; p. 2368, Ken King/Planet Earth Pictures; p. 2394, Hans Reinhard/ZEFA; p. 2420, Peter McDonald/ANT/NHPA; p. 2446, Stan Osolinski/Oxford Scientific Films

Published by Marshall Cavendish Corporation
99 White Plains Road
Tarrytown, New York 10591-9001

© Marshall Cavendish Corporation, 1997
© Marshall Cavendish Limited, 1994

The material in this series was first published in the English language by Marshall Cavendish Limited of 119 Wardour Street, London W1V 3TD, England.

Library of Congress Cataloging-in-Publication Data

Encyclopedia of mammals.
    p. cm.
    Includes index.
    ISBN 0-7614-0575-5 (set)   ISBN 0-7614-0576-3 (v. 1)

    Summary: Detailed articles cover the history, anatomy, feeding habits, social structure, reproduction, territory,
        and current status of ninety-five mammals around the world.
    1. Mammals—Encyclopedias, Juvenile. [1. Mammals—Encyclopedias.]   I. Marshall Cavendish Corporation.
    QL706.2.E54 1996
    599'.003—dc20   96-17736
                                                                                    CIP
                                                                                    AC

Printed in Malaysia
Bound in U.S.A.

CONTENTS

F.Lanting/ZEFA-Minden

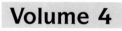

Illustration MC Picture Library

Illustration MC Picture Library

Volume 6

Volume 7

Volume 8

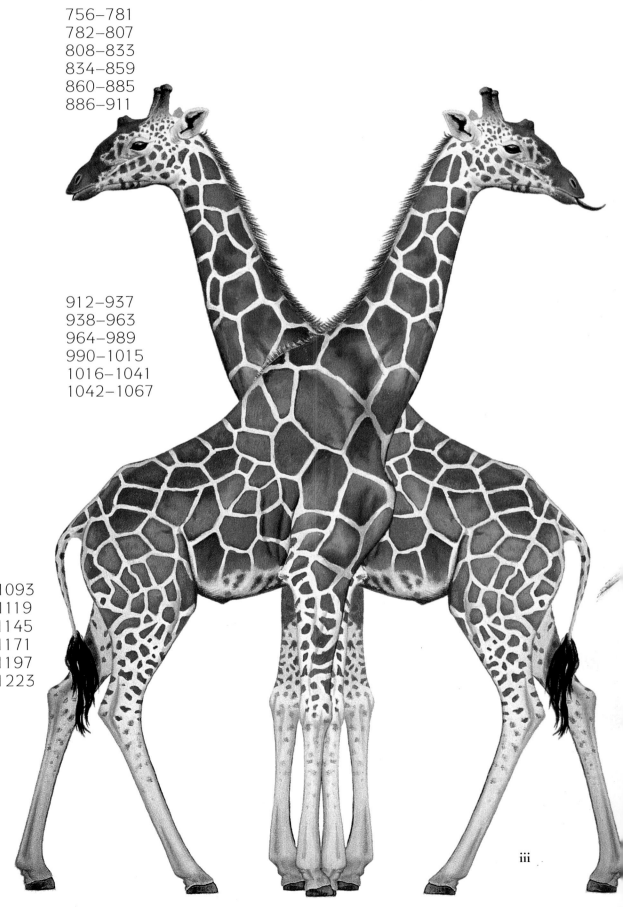

Illustration MC Picture Library

Illustration MC Picture Library

Volume 13

Volume 14

Volume 15

Illustration MC Picture Library

Volume 16

Volume 17

INTRODUCTION

THE LAST FEW MILLION YEARS ARE OFTEN CHARACTERIZED AS THE "AGE OF MAMMALS," PERHAPS NOT WITHOUT SOME BIAS SINCE HUMAN BEINGS FIND THEMSELVES IN THE CLASS MAMMALIA.

Objective examination of the current known diversity of life reveals that there are 9,000 birds, up to 19,000 fish, 250,000 higher plants, 750,000 insects (with some 290,000 beetles alone). We have only begun to count the microbiota, but there is every reason to believe that species numbers in this realm could be in the millions. Meanwhile, there are only some 4,000 mammals. This doesn't even exceed the reptiles and amphibians whose numbers amount to 6,300 and 4,200 respectively. The crowning of the dominant life form obviously depends a lot on the judges' view of success!

Nevertheless, mammals are indeed conspicuous and striking to the human eye and, for any number of reasons, will always be a major point of surprise and wonder. Now, with our ever-increasing ability to study mammals from the molecular to the anatomical to the psychological levels, an already fascinating story is unfolding to even higher adventure. Many of the latest findings are reported in these volumes, but like most investigations, every new answer generates a dozen new questions. Why are newborn bears born so tiny? What exactly is the relationship of whales to land mammals? How distinct are the three races of gorillas? What tips the balance toward sociality in lions but solitary living in most other cats? All readers will be fascinated with the mammal story, but the budding biologists and mammalogists will immediately recognize that all we know today is just a

Illustration MC Picture Library

Anup Shah/Planet Earth Pictures

scratch on the surface of the immense mystery surrounding all life on earth, including our closest kin, the other mammals.

There are many of us who would gladly pursue the questions and the mystery, but have been sidetracked into another field of biology: conservation biology. Species are dying out at an unprecedented rate, threatening to leave our planet scarred beyond human recognition. It has been calculated that nearly 25 percent of the 23,000 land vertebrates run the risk of becoming extinct within the next hundred years. A planet without elephants? Forests without tigers? Meadows without birdsong? Oceans without whales? These are all calculable possibilities that can easily be predicted based on current rates of direct persecution and habitat destruction. Extinction is indeed the

Earlier in this century, tigers numbered about 100,000 throughout their region. Today, less than 9,000 remain, and three subspecies are now extinct.

Michael McKavett/Bruce Coleman Ltd.

The sloth bear of Asia uses a unique suction action to feed primarily on termites.

outcome without direct human intervention to prevent it. Meanwhile, there are those who debate the importance of species diversity and rightly point out that a world without rhinoceroses is not a threat to human survival. But the list goes on, and at some point we must ask if the loss of so many of our kind—mammals and other vertebrates—might ultimately set the stage for the loss of the human mammal. We are all connected, from the smallest to the largest. Harvard's E. O. Wilson has reckoned that the loss of all insects would precede human extinction by only a matter of months because the loss of flower pollination and other miscellaneous functions would cause the collapse of the food chain we so depend upon.

The staggering increase of human numbers has set the stage for most of the wildlife crisis. It is intuitively easy to understand that if human beings are now using more and more space and resources, then there exists less space and fewer resources for wildlife. Figuring out what to do about it is far less intuitive. There is an interesting notion in popular mythology that nature is inexhaustible and that, for most of human history, wildlife and natural places could always be perceived as "somewhere else" if in fact they did not exist in the backyard. Now, humans are everywhere. If we don't find a way to protect and encourage nature all around us, it won't exist.

Conservation biology is still in its infancy, and new thinking in science, philosophy, and social psychology is coming to terms with the problem of disappearing wildlife. In the midst of almost daily tragedies in the decline of wildlife, glimmers of hope are emerging.

In the last few years, some impressive progress has been made. The black-footed ferret, believed to be extinct for several decades, was rediscovered in an isolated population just prior to a distemper epidemic that caused the population to crash to seventeen animals. Rescue of the seventeen animals, breeding, and subsequent reintroduction to at least two sites in the western United States have given the species a second chance while enhancing the sciences of captive breeding and population restoration at the same time. Zoological gardens have organized themselves to scientifically manage some of the most critically endangered species under the intensive protection of captivity, ranging from rhinoceroses to Lake Victoria cichlid fish and partula snails. The snails, many of the cichlid species, the Przhevalski's horse, the Père David deer, the Guam kingfisher, and the California condor would not exist were it not for the efforts of zoos. More recently, zoological gardens have begun to broaden their mission to include support of field biologists, nature preserves, and other wildlife conservation efforts around the world. Multifaceted programs of protection, research, and education are being designed to make a visit to the local zoo an act of international conservation.

Illustration MC Picture Library

Zebras, along with their relatives the horses and asses, are among the few survivors of a much larger horse family that arose millions of years ago.

The slow loris, a true primate and kin to monkeys and humans, is losing habitat due to farming and logging in its home in Southeast Asia.

At the other end of the spectrum, great foresight by governments and conservation organizations, such as the Wildlife Conservation Society, has been the operative in setting aside huge protected areas of many thousands of square miles in Tibet and western Africa, assuring relatively untouched wild spaces for whole ecosystems before population devastation occurs and heroic rescue becomes necessary. It is hoped that the Chang Tang Reserve of Tibet and the Nouabale N'Doki Reserve of Congo will continue to be bastions of wildlife spectacles well into the future.

Gerald Cubbitt/Bruce Coleman Ltd.

Art Wolfe/Tony Stone Worldwide

Meanwhile, it is clear that wildlife preserves need to be enhanced by programs that ensure that wildlife can survive outside of preserves and in close proximity to humans. The Cheetah Conservation Fund is a unique organization that has studied the survival needs of one of the beautiful large cats of Africa and is scientifically investigating the requirements for peaceful coexistence of Namibian farmers and the cheetah populations. The Peregrine Fund has established peregrine falcon populations in cities, and groups of small local school classes have cleaned up local streams or built nest boxes to encourage rare bird populations.

The precipitous decline of elephant numbers, due to a thriving illegal market in their ivory tusks, was brought under dramatic control in recent years with the ban of all ivory sales through CITES (Convention on International Trade in Endangered Species) and a continuing campaign to discourage the use of ivory. Although pressure to reopen a legal ivory trade continues, there is no real assurance that this would not once again create a conduit for illegal ivory and the

Whales include some of the largest creatures ever to exist on earth, but their survival has been threatened by commercial exploitation.

incentive for more mass slaughter. One of the great challenges of conservation biology in the twenty-first century will be to make "sustained harvest" of any wilderness product a viable term instead of the oxymoron it appears to be today. Ocean fisheries, timberlands, fresh water sources, and grazing lands have all been devastated for lack of the political will and scientific data to make them truly sustainable.

The leaders of the twenty-first century, many of whom are now the young readers of these volumes, will write the end of most of the wildlife-crisis chapters. Will the extinction crisis resolve as a triumph of human creativity, forethought, and ethics with a workable strategy for long-term survival of nature and all its colors? Or, is this the beginning of the end?

Dan Wharton

DIRECTOR OF THE CENTRAL PARK WILDLIFE CENTER,
WILDLIFE CONSERVATION SOCIETY

THE STORY OF
MAMMALS

WHAT MAKES A MAMMAL A MAMMAL?

THERE ARE THOUSANDS OF KINDS OF MAMMALS,
INCLUDING HUMANS, THAT LIVE ALL OVER THE WORLD,
HIGH UP IN THE TREES AND DEEP UNDER THE SEA,
IN THE BLAZING DESERT AND THE FREEZING TUNDRA

Despite their diversity, all mammals share certain characteristics
which, taken together, set them apart from other animals. They
all have mammary glands, which are the organs used by the
females to feed milk to their young and from which they get
their name.

KEEPING WARM

All mammals are warm-blooded or endothermic, which
means they can maintain a regular internal body temperature
using the heat generated in their muscles and other body
tissues. These changes in temperature are monitored and
regulated by the brain.

Mammals have hair or fur to retain this heat and keep them
warm in cold weather. Many have fur all over their bodies,
and some over parts of their bodies, while some mammals, such
as whales, have only a few hairs. Many mammals handle hot
temperatures with active sweat glands that release water from
the bloodstream onto the surface of the skin which evaporates

and cools the body. (A few mammals have no sweat glands
and cool down by panting, conducting interior body heat
outward through the mouth.)

Mammals have four limbs (in some sea mammals these
have become flippers), well-developed brains, and efficient
hearts with four separate chambers, which separate fresh
from used blood.

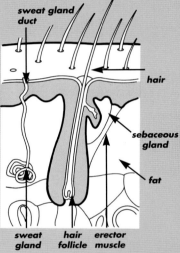

sweat gland
duct

hair

sebaceous
gland

fat

sweat   hair   erector
gland   follicle muscle

SKIN AND HAIR

*Hair grows from sacs or follicles
attached to erector muscles,
which can cause the hair to
stand on end. Sebaceous glands
produce an oily substance that
waterproofs the hair and skin,
while sweat glands produce
sweat, which evaporates to
cool the body. Some mammals'
hair is made up of two layers:
a fine undercoat, which
provides insulation by trapping
air, and longer guard hairs
for waterproofing.*

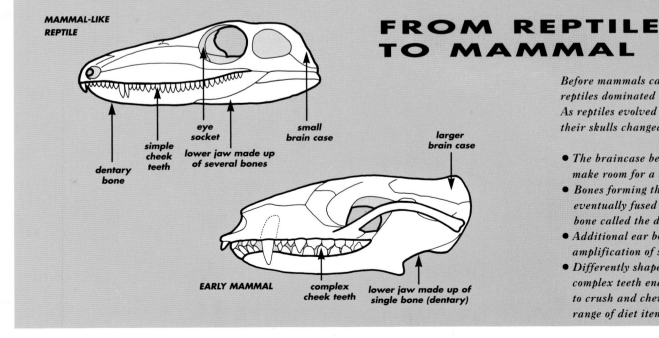

MAMMAL-LIKE
REPTILE

dentary
bone

simple
cheek
teeth

eye
socket

lower jaw made up
of several bones

small
brain case

EARLY MAMMAL

complex
cheek teeth

lower jaw made up of
single bone (dentary)

larger
brain case

FROM REPTILE TO MAMMAL

*Before mammals came along,
reptiles dominated the earth.
As reptiles evolved into mammals,
their skulls changed:*

- *The braincase became larger to
  make room for a bigger brain.*
- *Bones forming the lower jaw
  eventually fused into one strong
  bone called the dentary.*
- *Additional ear bones gave better
  amplification of sound waves.*
- *Differently shaped, more
  complex teeth enabled mammals
  to crush and chew a wide
  range of diet items.*

MAMMAL GROUPS

here are three types of mammals, which differ in the ways they produce and nourish their young:

MONOTREME

he monotremes are the most primitive of the ree types of mammals, the ones most osely resembling their reptilian ncestors. Like reptiles they lay gs that are incubated in a nest or the mother's pouch and are ourished through the egg yolk. nlike reptiles, though, when e eggs are hatched the oung are nourished with e milk that oozes from ts in the mother's skin.

Monotreme egg (above left); *short-beaked echidna nursing* (left and above).

MARSUPIAL

Kangaroos and other marsupials do not lay eggs. Infants are born at an early stage, after a short gestation period, and immediately crawl blindly into the pouch (or marsupium) on their mother's abdomen. Here they attach themselves to a nipple and finish their development, nourished by the milk that flows from her mammary glands.

Kangaroo with young in pouch (left); *newborn kangaroo* (right).

PLACENTAL

acental embryos remain in the mother's body til they are well developed. This is possible cause they receive nourishment from an organ lled the placenta, which allows d and oxygen to pass from the other's bloodstream to the oodstream of the developing bryo, without the two oodstreams actually mixing. e length of time the young main in the womb varies ughly according to body size.

Placental embryo in mother's womb (left); *kittens nursing* (above).

Illustrations Malcolm Spice/Black Hat

Des & Jen Bartlett/Survival Anglia

J. Paul Ferrero/Ardea

Hans Reinhard/Bruce Coleman Ltd.

John Cancalosi/Bruce Coleman Ltd.

WHAT IS EVOLUTION?

Until Charles Darwin published a book called *On the Origin of Species* in 1859, people believed that animals had always looked the way they do now, with no new species appearing since the Creation. But Darwin realized that, when animals breed, they produce more offspring than the environment can support.

These offspring vary slightly from each other and from their parents, and some are better suited, or adapted, to the conditions at the time. For example, a long-haired animal is better adapted to a cold climate than a short-haired one.

Fossil of an extinct lobsterlike creature called a trilobite.

So the long-haired animal has a better chance of surviving to mate with another long-haired animal, and this pair would produce long-haired offspring. A short-haired animal, on the other hand, is more likely to die of cold before it has a chance of reproducing. This is known as "survival of the fittest."

Darwin based his theories on the fossils he studied, and people have continued studying fossils to this day. All the animals shown on pages xviii–xix have been discovered as a result of fossil finds.

HOW DID MAMMALS EVOLVE?

ALTHOUGH THE FIRST ANIMALS—
VERY SIMPLE, SINGLE-CELLED CREATURES
THAT LIVED IN THE SEAS—CAME
INTO BEING ABOUT 1.2 BILLION
YEARS AGO, IT TOOK SOME 1 BILLION
YEARS FOR MAMMALS TO MAKE
THEIR FIRST APPEARANCE.

In the interim came the move from water
to land: Fish evolved into amphibians,
which evolved into reptiles. Some of these
evolved into mammals via a group of
intermediate animals called mammal-like
reptiles, and some evolved into dinosaurs.

ALL CHANGE

In the meantime the mammals were
diversifying, and four groups formed: the
placentals, marsupials, and monotremes
all survive today, while the rodentlike
multituberculates became extinct. The
highly successful placentals evolved in
different ways to form 21 groups (see
pages xx–xxi).

The evolution of life on earth was
influenced by major changes to the planet.
Major upheavals under the earth's surface
caused the continents to move together,
then to split apart. This caused the climate
to go through dramatic changes and, as a
result, plant and animal life changed too.

MAMMAL-LIKE REPTILES **MAMMALS**

CYNOGNATHUS

About 40 in (100 cm) long,
Cynognathus (sin-og-NAY-
thus) had a very large head.
More like a mammal than a
reptile, it was probably
furry, with mammal-like
teeth, which gave it a
ferocious bite, and hind
limbs tucked under its body.

MORGANUCODON

A long-snouted creature
only 1 in (2–3 cm) long,
Morganucodon
(mor-gan-YOOK-oh-don)
was probably the first true
mammal. It came out at
night to hunt for food,
which consisted of insects,
worms, and young reptiles.

CRUSAFONTIA

*The two major continents of
Euramerica and Gondwanaland,
plus three smaller landmasses,
had come together 210 million
years ago to form a single
landmass called Pangaea. At
this point in time animals could
easily spread over wide areas.*

THE CHANGING LANDSCAPE

IN THE BEGINNING

For billions of years the seas covered much
of the earth. Life began here in the form of
primitive marine plants and wormlike animals.
Plant and animal life evolved and, eventually,
moved onto land.

TRIASSIC

In the 40 or so million years known as the
Triassic period, many inland areas became
covered with desert in the warm, dry climate.
Reptiles were the dominant animal, with new
types, including dinosaurs and large marine
reptiles, evolving. In this period the first
mammals made their appearance.

JURASSIC

The climate became more humid and cycads,
ferns, and conifers were abundant in this Age
of Dinosaurs. The first birds appeared, though
the skies were dominated by pterosaurs or
flying reptiles, and marine reptiles such as
ichthyosaurs roamed the seas.

240 million years ago   **200**   **140**

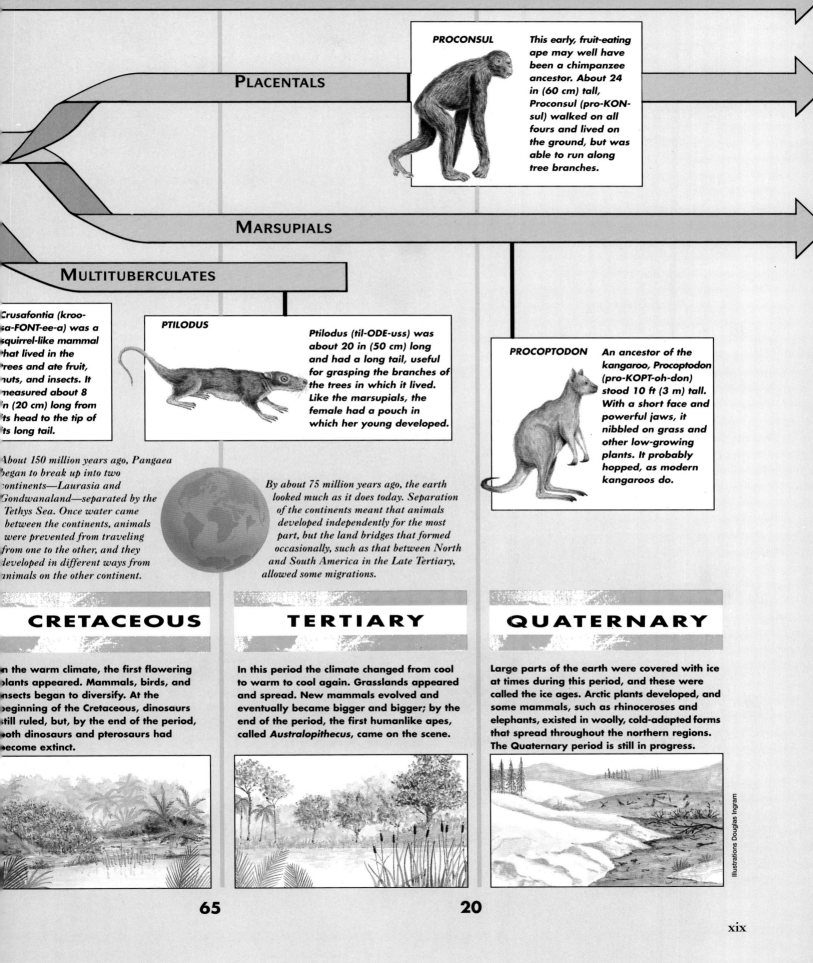

MONOTREMES

PLACENTALS

PROCONSUL

This early, fruit-eating ape may well have been a chimpanzee ancestor. About 24 in (60 cm) tall, Proconsul (pro-KON-sul) walked on all fours and lived on the ground, but was able to run along tree branches.

MARSUPIALS

MULTITUBERCULATES

Crusafontia (kroo-sa-FONT-ee-a) was a squirrel-like mammal that lived in the trees and ate fruit, nuts, and insects. It measured about 8 in (20 cm) long from its head to the tip of its long tail.

PTILODUS

Ptilodus (til-ODE-uss) was about 20 in (50 cm) long and had a long tail, useful for grasping the branches of the trees in which it lived. Like the marsupials, the female had a pouch in which her young developed.

PROCOPTODON

An ancestor of the kangaroo, Procoptodon (pro-KOPT-oh-don) stood 10 ft (3 m) tall. With a short face and powerful jaws, it nibbled on grass and other low-growing plants. It probably hopped, as modern kangaroos do.

About 150 million years ago, Pangaea began to break up into two continents—Laurasia and Gondwanaland—separated by the Tethys Sea. Once water came between the continents, animals were prevented from traveling from one to the other, and they developed in different ways from animals on the other continent.

By about 75 million years ago, the earth looked much as it does today. Separation of the continents meant that animals developed independently for the most part, but the land bridges that formed occasionally, such as that between North and South America in the Late Tertiary, allowed some migrations.

CRETACEOUS

In the warm climate, the first flowering plants appeared. Mammals, birds, and insects began to diversify. At the beginning of the Cretaceous, dinosaurs still ruled, but, by the end of the period, both dinosaurs and pterosaurs had become extinct.

TERTIARY

In this period the climate changed from cool to warm to cool again. Grasslands appeared and spread. New mammals evolved and eventually became bigger and bigger; by the end of the period, the first humanlike apes, called *Australopithecus*, came on the scene.

QUATERNARY

Large parts of the earth were covered with ice at times during this period, and these were called the ice ages. Arctic plants developed, and some mammals, such as rhinoceroses and elephants, existed in woolly, cold-adapted forms that spread throughout the northern regions. The Quaternary period is still in progress.

65   20

WHAT KINDS OF MAMMALS

ALL THE MAMMALS LIVING TODAY CAN BE DIVIDED INTO 21 GROUPS OR ORDERS:

MONOTREMES
Monotremata

There are three species of monotremes: the platypus and the short- and long-beaked echidnas. The most primitive of the mammal orders, monotremes have many similarities with birds and reptiles and are the sole mammals that lay eggs. They are found only in Australasia.

MONOTREMES

MARSUPIALS
Marsupialia

Marsupials, which include kangaroos, koalas, and wombats, are distinguished by their unique reproductive system, including a pouch called the marsupium. They are found in the Americas as well as in Australasia.

MARSUPIALS

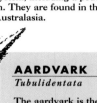

AARDVARK
Tubulidentata

The aardvark is the only species to have an order all to itself, though it is distantly related to both the elephant and the hyrax. This secretive mammal is found in Africa and looks like a long-eared, long-snouted pig.

PLACENTAL

ANTEATERS, SLOTHS, AND ARMADILLOS
Edentata

These mammals have either no teeth or a few simple ones and a specially strengthened backbone that is unique to the order. They are found in South and Central America, southern Asia, and Africa, and are also known as the Xenartha.

PLACENTAL

BATS
Chiroptera

Bats are the only mammals that can fly; their wings are made of a very fine membrane. There are two suborders, roughly divided between bats that eat fruit and bats that eat insects. They are found worldwide, except for the polar regions.

PLACENTAL

CARNIVORES
Carnivora

This order of flesh-eating mammals includes cats, dogs, bears, raccoons, weasels, civets, and hyenas. They all have four bladelike teeth called carnassials, which they use to tear meat. Carnivores are found all over the world.

PLACENTAL

ELEPHANTS
Proboscidea

Found in parts of Africa and southern Asia, elephants are the largest living land mammals. Their long trunks are used to pick up vegetation from the ground or from tall trees, as well as for smelling, drinking, and communicating.

PLACENTAL

xx

ELEPHANT SHREWS
Macroscelidea

These long-legged, long-tailed mammals, of which there are 15 species, are found only in certain parts of Africa. They have long snouts, which they use to forage for invertebrates.

PLACENTAL

EVEN-TOED HOOFED MAMMALS
Artiodactyla

This order, also known as the even-toed ungulates, is distributed all over the world, except for Australasia and Antarctica. It includes pigs, hippos, camels, deer, giraffes, antelope, cattle, sheep, and goats.

PLACENTAL

FLYING LEMURS
Dermoptera

There are only two species of flying lemurs (also known as colugos), found only in Southeast Asia. They do not actually fly but have a large membrane that stretches from the neck, along the fingers and toes, to the tip of the tail, which they use for gliding.

PLACENTAL

HYRAXES
Hyracoidea

These rabbit-sized mammals look similar to guinea pigs, but they are, in fact, more closely related to elephants and aardvarks than rodents. Also called dassies, they are found in Africa and the Middle East.

PLACENTAL

INSECTIVORES
Insectivora

Although insectivores are primarily insect-eating mammals, in fact their diet also includes worms and fish. They include shrews, hedgehogs, and moles, and are found in Europe, Asia, Africa, and North and Central America.

PLACENTAL

ODD-TOED HOOFED MAMMALS
Perissodactyla

This order, which includes horses, zebras, tapirs, and rhinos, is also called the odd-toed ungulates, as all the species have an odd number of toes. They are found in Africa, Asia, and Central and South America.

PLACENTAL

PANGOLINS
Pholidota

Found in southern Asia and Africa, pangolins, or scaly anteaters, are medium-sized mammals covered all over with large, horny, overlapping brown scales. They curl up into balls to protect themselves.

PLACENTAL

PRIMATES
Primates

Primates, which include monkeys, lemurs, apes, and humans, all have flexible hands and feet with grasping thumbs and toes. Nonhuman primates are found in South and Central America, southern Asia, and Africa.

PLACENTAL

RABBITS, HARES, AND PIKAS
Lagomorpha

These mammals all possess short tails and two pairs of upper incisors for gnawing at vegetation. Found worldwide except for Antarctica, they live in a wide variety of habitats.

PLACENTAL

RODENTS
Rodentia

With over 1,700 species, rodents are the most abundant of the mammals. Found in every habitat all over the world, they feed on plants and small invertebrates, which they eat with the help of their long, razor-sharp incisors.

PLACENTAL

SEA COWS AND MANATEES
Sirenia

These plant-eating aquatic mammals—three species of manatees and one dugong—look like seals but share an ancestor with the elephant. They are found around the coasts and rivers of the Americas, Africa, Asia, and Australasia.

PLACENTAL

SEALS AND SEA LIONS
Pinnipedia

This order (also known as the pinnipeds or wing-footed mammals) includes the walrus and consists of carnivorous aquatic mammals that breed and give birth on land. They are found in coastal waters all over the world.

PLACENTAL

TREE SHREWS
Scandentia

Tree shrews are small, squirrel-like mammals with pointed noses and long tails. Found only in southern and Southeast Asia, they live in tropical rain forests, on the ground as well as in trees. In the past, some zoologists grouped them together with the primates.

PLACENTAL

WHALES AND DOLPHINS
Cetacea

Whales, dolphins, and porpoises, also known as cetaceans, live in every ocean of the world, as well as in some rivers. They breathe air through blowholes and have streamlined bodies, flippers, and flattened tails for swimming.

PLACENTAL

HOW ARE ANIMALS CLASSIFIED?

Zoologists group all animals (and botanists group plants) into different categories in order to show how they are related to each other. These categories are known by their Latin names so that people around the world can recognize them.

This system of classification, called taxonomy, starts by dividing all animals into those with backbones and those without, then breaks these down further and further into related groups until you get to the species, which is defined as a population of animals that are capable of breeding with each other and producing fertile offspring.

As well as the divisions shown below, there may be additional ones such as suborders, superfamilies, and subspecies.

THIS IS HOW A VAMPIRE BAT IS CLASSIFIED:

KINGDOM
Animalia
(Latin for "animals")
▼
PHYLUM
Chordata
(animals with backbones)
▼
CLASS
Mammalia
(mammals)
▼
ORDER
Chiroptera
(all bats)
▼
FAMILY
Desmodontidae
(includes three types of vampire bats)
▼
GENUS
Desmodus
▼
SPECIES
rotundus

Animals are known to scientists by two-word names, which consist of the genus (spelled with an initial capital letter) followed by the species (with a lower-case letter), so the vampire bat is known as *Desmodus rotundus* (genus and species are always italicized).

WHERE DO MAMMALS LIVE?

Millions of years ago, when there was only one central landmass, all animals could move around more or less freely. But, as the continents gradually split apart, they took with them the animals living there. These animals then evolved in their own ways in their new environments, some becoming extinct and some thriving. Later, when some of the continents temporarily joined up again, animals could move over these land bridges to new homes.

Scientists have divided the present-day world into six different regions called zoogeographic regions, each with its own distinctive animal life.

NEARCTIC REGION

At different points in the past, this region was joined to both the Neotropical and the Palearctic regions, so it shares some of their animal life. However, two mammals are unique to the region: the pronghorn antelope and the mountain beaver.

PALEARCTIC REGION

Though it is the largest in area of the zoogeographic regions and has a wide range of mammals, the Palearctic region has only two unique families, both rodents, namely the blind mole rats and the desert dormouse.

ORIENTAL REGION

This region shares much of its animal life—including the rhinoceros, elephant, some apes, and the pangolin—with the Ethiopian region, but the tarsiers, tree shrews, flying lemurs, and spiny dormouse are unique.

NEOTROPICAL REGION

This region, almost as isolated as the Australian region, has many of its own mammals, including anteaters, sloths, and armadillos, some species of opossum, monkeys such as marmosets and tamarins, and rodents such as the chinchilla.

ETHIOPIAN REGION

The gorilla, the chimp, the giraffe, the hippopotamus, and the aardvark are found only in this region, as are certain species of rodents. Worth noting, the island of Madagascar has its own peculiar animal life, in particular the lemurs.

AUSTRALIAN REGION

This region has been isolated for over 50 million years, and, as a result, many of the mammals living elsewhere never reached it. Thus it has its own unique mammals—the marsupials—of which the best known is the kangaroo.

READER'S GUIDE

Encyclopedia of Mammals is an essential key to the lives and futures of the world's mammals. Each entry focuses on a different mammal or group of mammals and contains three easy-to-follow sections—PROFILE, BEHAVIOR, and SURVIVAL—which together provide all the information you will ever need on the animal kingdom.

PROFILE

PROFILE PROVIDES AN INTRODUCTORY PORTRAIT OF THE ANIMAL:

- TELLS YOU WHAT IT LOOKS LIKE—INSIDE AND OUT
- DESCRIBES THE DIFFERENT VARIETIES OF THE ANIMAL
- TELLS YOU ABOUT ITS CLOSE RELATIONS AND ITS ANCESTORS

SPECIAL FEATURES:

CLASSIFICATION PANELS take you through the scientific subdivisions used to classify each mammal.
FAMILY TREES show how mammals are related. Pronunciation keys help with Latin names.
ANCESTORS looks at the prehistoric creatures that were the early relations of present-day mammals.

BEHAVIOR

BEHAVIOR INVESTIGATES ALL ASPECTS OF THE ANIMAL'S LIFE, FROM HOW IT RAISES ITS YOUNG TO THE WAYS IN WHICH IT DEFENDS ITS TERRITORY. IN EACH ENTRY, A SELECTION OF THE FOLLOWING TOPICS IS COVERED:

- HABITATS ● HUNTING ● FOOD AND FEEDING
- REPRODUCTION ● TERRITORY ● SOCIAL STRUCTURE
- LIFE CYCLE ● HIBERNATION ● SOCIAL MIGRATION

SPECIAL FEATURES:

KEY FACTS provide quick reference information about each mammal.
INSIGHT looks at particularly interesting aspects of life in the animal world.
FOCUS ON examines the featured animal in a specific habitat.

SURVIVAL

SURVIVAL LOOKS AT HOW AND WHY ANIMALS ARE UNDER THREAT AND WHAT—IF ANYTHING—THE NATIONS OF THE WORLD ARE DOING TO SAVE THEM. THIS SECTION ALSO INVESTIGATES THOSE SPECIES THAT CONTINUE TO FLOURISH.

SPECIAL FEATURES:

THEN AND NOW shows how the animal landscape has altered over the years.
ALONGSIDE MAN investigates the different aspects of the relationship between humans and mammals.
INTO THE FUTURE considers the animal's prospects and makes predictions about its future.

AARDVARKS

RELATIONS

The aardvark and hyraxes belong to orders of their own. Their closest living relatives include:

ELEPHANTS

MANATEES

DUGONG

Patti Murray/Oxford Scientific Films

The aardvark and the hyraxes belong to two mammal orders: the Tubulidentata, which contains only the aardvark, and the Hyracoidea, which consists of just one family, three genera, and twelve species.

ORDER

Tubulidentata
(aardvark)

FAMILY

Orycteropodidae

GENUS AND SPECIES

Oryceropus afer

ORDER

Hyracoidea
(hyraxes)

FAMILY

Procaviidae

GENUS

Procavia
(rock hyraxes)
five species

Heterohyrax
(bush hyraxes)
four species

Dendrohyrax
(tree hyraxes)
three species

STRANGER THAN FICTION

ALONG WITH ELEPHANTS, SEA COWS, AND HYRAXES, THE AARDVARK IS A PRIMITIVE-HOOFED MAMMAL. MOST PECULIAR IN APPEARANCE, IT IS A SURVIVOR FROM A FORGOTTEN PAGE IN NATURE'S HISTORY BOOK

I f the aardvark were a fictitious animal, the product of someone's fertile imagination, most people would probably dismiss it as being too improbable to exist. With its near-naked skin, huge ears, long piglike snout, and disproportionately large rear end, it looks as though it comes from a book about mythical creatures. And yet this strange animal does exist and until recently was quite common in the southern part of the African continent.

Hyraxes look like the American cavies, which is why, in 1870, their family was named Procaviidae. The two groups are not at all related, but the name has stuck. Fossil evidence has shown that the hyraxes are, amazingly, more closely related to elephants than any other group. They and the aardvark are primitive-hoofed mammals whose origins can be traced back to a now-extinct mammal order called the Condylarths, which first appeared some seventy million years ago.

3

About sixty million years ago a group of Condylarths called the Phenacodontids (fenna-co-DON-tidz) appeared. These were the forerunners of the horses and other odd-toed ungulates (hoofed mammals), and included the horselike *Phenacodus*. Among the descendants of *Phenacodus* and its relatives are hyraxes, elephants, aardvark, manatees, and dugong. Of all these, the aardvark is probably the nearest living relative of the extinct condylarths.

A ONE-OF-A-KIND ANTEATER

The aardvark is a termite-eating specialist, and naturalists formerly classified it in the Edentate order, along with sloths, anteaters, armadillos, and pangolins. But the similarities of this animal to anteaters are not due to any relationship; they are simply the result of parallel evolution. The two groups adapted to a similar lifestyle and have thus evolved similar forms. The idea of any direct

Stephen Dalton/NHPA

Hyraxes (above) *are highly alert, with keen senses, and are quick to respond to danger.*

Hermann Brehm/Bruce Coleman Ltd.

MISLEADING NAMES

The modern names of many animals reflect past zoological confusion, and the names given to the aardvark and the hyraxes are perhaps classic examples. *Hyrax* is derived from the Greek word *hurax,* which means "shrew mouse." *Aardvark* is an Afrikaans word meaning "earth pig," which refers simply to the animal's piglike snout and its ability to dig rapidly into the ground. The alternative name for this animal, "antbear," demonstrates confusion not only between ants and termites—which is relatively easy to understand—but also between aardvarks and bears!

To many people, however, these names may seem entirely reasonable, based as they are on the appearance of the animals in question. To such people, the truth may seem a little too fantastic. It may be hard to believe that the aardvark and the hyraxes are actually related to hoofed mammals and that their closest relatives are elephants and sea cows, but this is what zoologists and scientists are telling us!

relationship has now been abandoned, and today the aardvark is classified all by itself in the mammal order Tubulidentata.

This name means "tube teeth." Each of the aardvark's teeth consists of many hexagonal prisms of dentine that surround tubular pulp cavities; the second molar—the largest of the aardvark's teeth—contains 1,500 of these prisms. Since they are continually being worn down by hard-shelled insects and gritty soil, the column-shaped teeth grow throughout the animal's life.

THE ENIGMATIC HYRAXES

The relationships of hyraxes have been the subject of much argument. Two extinct families are known, but there is no fossil evidence of their early ancestry. Certainly, by about forty million years ago, they had become so well established that they were the most important medium-sized browsers and grazers in Africa. There were at least six genera, representing several different evolutionary lines.

About twenty-five million years ago hyraxes fell into decline; they could not compete with the bovids (the cattle family) that were then spreading

Sunbathing is an important morning ritual for hyraxes. It helps restore their body warmth.

through Africa. The only hyraxes that survived there were those that lived in places where they did not compete with bovids—that is, among the rocks or in trees. Within the last five million years, however, hyraxes spread, presumably ahead of the antelopes and cattle, into the Mediterranean region of Europe and into Asia as far as China, where they survived until the last few thousand years.

Today there are three genera left, but as there are no known fossils of these living genera, their origins, like those of the early hyraxes, are a matter of some speculation. There is, however, little doubt that they did have a common ancestor that walked on the soles of its feet instead of on hooves. Modern hyraxes are probably dwarf forms of their ancestors—the degree to which the toes on the sides of the feet have degenerated shows that their ancestors were, like all hoofed animals, good runners.

Scientists cannot even agree about the classification of modern hyraxes, other than distinguishing between tree, bush, and rock species. Tree hyraxes, of which there are three species, are recognized as belonging to the genus *Dendrohyrax*. Bush hyraxes belong to the genus *Heterohyrax*, but opinions differ as to the number and naming of the species in this group, and in at least one classification this genus contains four out of the five species that are normally placed in the rock hyrax genus *Procavia*.

Hyraxes are small, squat animals, about the size of hares or marmots. They crouch like rabbits, for which they have often been mistaken in the past. Species that live in warm dry regions have short fur, while tree hyraxes and those that live in mountainous regions have thick, soft fur. ∎

(A)NCESTORS

The best, if not the oldest, hyrax fossils come from the Fayum beds in Egypt, dating from the Oligocene epoch (38–25 million years ago). Among the animals of that time was *Geniohyus* (jee-nee-o-HIE-us), a long-snouted animal with three-toed feet. *Sagatherium* (sa-ga-THEE-re-um) was a short-snouted animal more like modern hyraxes. *Megalohyrax* (mega-lo-HIE-racks) also had three toes, and, as its name implies, was a large animal when compared with modern hyraxes. Later hyraxes included *Postschizotherium* (post-skitz-o-THEE-re-um) and *Gigantohyrax* (jy-gant-o-HIE-racks), which were the size of donkeys.

B/W illustrations Ruth Grewcock

THE AARDVARK'S AND HYRAXES' FAMILY TREE

This family tree shows how scientists believe that aardvarks and hyraxes may be related. A common ancestor is presumed to have existed among the primitive-hoofed animals known as the Condylarths, and the aardvark is thought to be the closest living relative of this group. Another line of ungulates is thought to have given rise to the hyraxes, together with the elephants and manatees and sea cow (dugong).

TREE HYRAXES
Dendrohyrax
(den-dro-HIE-racks)

There are three species of tree hyraxes, found in wooded regions of Africa. They are nocturnal and live in trees. One species, found in the Ruwenzori Mountains in Uganda, also lives on the ground, since there are no other hyraxes in its local habitat.

PRIMITIVE UNGULATES

ELEPHANTS

CONDYLARTHA

ROCK HYRAX
Procavia
(pro-CAH-vee-ah)

There are five species of rock hyraxes—at least, according to most scientists. These creatures have a compact form with no visible tail. Their rubbery, sweaty toe pads have a remarkably good grip upon the rocky outcrops, or kopjes (COP-eez), of their native home on the African plains. Rock hyraxes are highly social animals that live in stable family groups. In parts of their range where natural predators have been eliminated by humans, rock hyraxes have become an agricultural pest.

BUSH HYRAX
Heterohyrax
(hetter-o-HIE-racks)

There are from two to four species of bush hyraxes, depending on the method of classification. They live in rocky outcrops in southern and eastern Africa, where they often mingle with the rock hyraxes. In fact, they often huddle together with their rock-living cousins, especially in the sunlight of the early morning.

HYRAXES

AARDVARK
Orycteropus afer
(ORR-ick-teh-rope-uss AFF-er)

The extraordinary aardvark seems an unlikely kind of animal, but it is in fact a successful predator on the abundant termites of the African savanna. Despite having a reasonably healthy population status, the elusive aardvark is rarely seen and even today remains something of an enigma.

Color illustrations Carol Roberts

DUGONG AND MANATEES

ANATOMY: THE AARDVARK

HYRAX FOREFOOT   HIND FOOT

A hyrax walks on its soles. Naked toe pads, moistened by special glands, grip rocks or bark very tightly. A muscle in the center of each pad draws the center in so that it forms a suction cup.

THE EARS

are long and tubelike, and the skin is smooth and waxy. The aardvark can move them independently of one another, and when it is digging it folds them back to keep dirt out.

The aardvark (above left) measures up to 63 in (160 cm) long and may weigh as much as 180 lb (82 kg), although most individuals weigh 110–154 lb (50–70 kg). Hyraxes (above right) measure 12–25 in (30–63 cm) from head to tail and weigh up to 12 lb (5.4 kg). The tail is only 0.4–1.2 in (1–3 cm) long, or is lacking altogether.

EACH EYE

contains a special membrane—the umbraculum—that acts as a shade for the pupil and allows the animal to sit motionless on a rock apparently gazing directly at the sun.

NOSTRILS

On the tip of the snout are two circular nostrils from which grow a number of whitish, curved hairs, each 1–2 in (22–50 mm) long. The nostrils can be sealed shut to keep out soil when digging.

THE TONGUE

is long and tapering and is often left hanging outside the mouth, with the end coiled up like a clock spring.

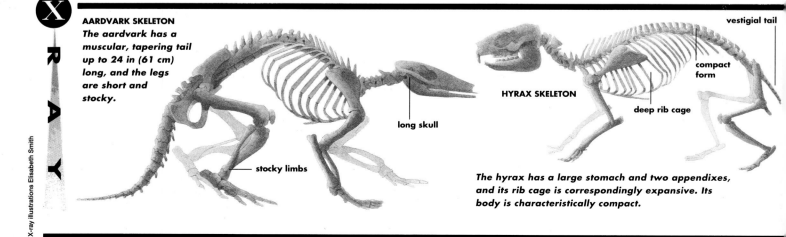

X RAY

AARDVARK SKELETON
The aardvark has a muscular, tapering tail up to 24 in (61 cm) long, and the legs are short and stocky.

stocky limbs

long skull

HYRAX SKELETON

vestigial tail

compact form

deep rib cage

The hyrax has a large stomach and two appendixes, and its rib cage is correspondingly expansive. Its body is characteristically compact.

X-ray illustrations Elisabeth Smith

HYRAX

CLASSIFICATION

GENUS: *ORYCTEROPUS*

SPECIES: *AFER*

SIZE

**HEAD–BODY LENGTH: 40–63 IN
(100–160 CM)**

WEIGHT: 110–155 LB (50–70 KG)

COLORATION

PINKISH GRAY SKIN WITH A SPARSE COVERING OF HAIR THAT VARIES IN COLOR FROM BROWN TO YELLOWISH GRAY

FEATURES

LONG SNOUT ENDING IN A PIGLIKE MUZZLE

LARGE, WAXY, NAKED EARS

LARGE HINDQUARTERS, SEEMINGLY OUT OF PROPORTION TO THE REST OF THE BODY

TAPERING TAIL

TREE HYRAX HIND FOOT

The feet are well padded. The tree hyrax is a skilled climber, and its hind foot can be revolved on its axis.

THE TAIL

tapers away from a stout base with a circumference of about 16 in (40 cm). It often leaves a distinctive trail on soft ground.

THE CLAWS

are long, slightly curved, and spoon shaped, with sharp edges for digging. There are four claws on the forefeet and five on the hind feet.

AARDVARK TEETH

no incisors or canines

The skull is long and narrow with simple dentition; there are only about five flat, rootless cheek teeth on each side of each jaw. There are no incisors or canines.

AARDVARK SKULL

The teeth are tubular, and each is made up of many long, six-sided tubes of dentine. The tooth is surrounded by a layer of cementlike material instead of enamel.

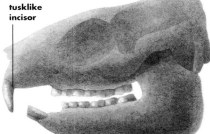

tusklike incisor

HYRAX SKULL

The hyrax first grows milk teeth—12 incisors and a canine tooth in the upper jaw. With the arrival of permanent molars, only one incisor is left in the upper jaw and no canines remain.

LIFE ON THE ROCKS

WHILE THE AARDVARK IS A SOLITARY, NOCTURNAL, AND SECRETIVE ANTEATER, THE HYRAXES ARE THE COMPLETE OPPOSITE: THEY BASK OR HUDDLE IN LIVELY, CHATTERING GROUPS ON ROCKY OUTCROPS

The aardvark lives alone or in pairs and spends the day relaxing inside its burrow, partly to avoid predators and partly to escape the heat of the sun. It rarely leaves its burrow before nightfall. It peers out cautiously at first, sniffing the air and listening with its huge ears for the slightest sound. If, at this stage, all seems safe, it leaps out and takes a thorough look at its surroundings. When satisfied that there is no danger, it calms down and begins the important task of finding food. During the night an aardvark may travel 1–19 miles (2–30 km) in its search for termites, depending on how plentiful they are. As it searches for its food, it makes soft grunting noises, which become much louder as the animal prepares to disappear into a burrow.

BODY HEAT

An aardvark has no fat under its skin and therefore cannot easily conserve body heat. But this is not much of a problem, as, even in daytime temperatures of 86°F (30°C) or more, the aardvark's burrow stays at a more or less constant 75°F (24°C)—roughly equivalent to the normal night temperature.

Hyraxes, too, cannot control their body temperature, but in their case this is more of a problem. In the morning, they must emerge from their lairs soon after dawn and spend several hours basking in the sun before they can start to feed. During the hottest hours they have to seek shade, so feeding is limited to cooler times, generally toward evening.

Tree hyraxes, like aardvarks, are solitary and nocturnal. Rock and bush hyraxes, however, may be active at any time, and live in colonies that contain anything from a few to several hundred individuals. Often, individuals of different species, or even of different genera, can be found occupying the same pile of rocks. They even bask in the sun together and huddle up on cooler days.

Rock and bush hyraxes communicate in screams, whistles, and chatters; at least 21 calls have been recognized. While a group feeds, one animal—usually a senior male—keeps watch. If danger threatens, this lookout gives the alarm, at which all the others rush for cover. The calls vary among species, but different species will respond to each other's alarm signals. Hyraxes are also very agile climbers and jumpers: They are the only ungulates that can climb smooth trees and rocks.

Ever alert, hyrax family groups post a sentry (above) *to keep watch for perils such as eagles.*

Joan Root/Survival Anglia

DEATH ON THE ROCK

The hyraxes' main enemy is the verreaux eagle. This bird prefers dry country and is found in mountains, desert scrub, and savanna, and its habitat therefore coincides almost exactly with that of hyraxes.

This small black eagle has a wingspan of about 24 in (60 cm), and it soars easily through the air with hardly a wing beat, often spending hours without hunting. When it does decide to kill, it plunges like a stone toward its prey. Some 80 percent of its food consists of mammals, and its staple quarry is the rock hyrax. However, it also preys upon hares, dik-diks, partridges, guinea fowl, reptiles, and even a few carnivores, such as mongooses.

The piercing calls of male tree hyraxes are probably the most striking of all hyrax noises. A single call may last up to five minutes and contain up to 130 individual cries. The cries start quietly as a series of croaks and build up to a crescendo of screams, until they suddenly stop. In the rain forest, it is often only the last 30 to 40 screams that are heard, as the quieter noises are absorbed by vegetation. The calls are used as territorial markers and allow opposite sexes to locate each other. Each animal usually calls twice each night. ∎

Occasionally, after a particularly cold night, aardvarks may be seen basking in the sun.

HABITATS

Because the aardvark is so dependent on termites for its food, it is limited to those places where termites can survive. Fortunately for the aardvark, termites are found in a wide range of habitats; this mammal is therefore found throughout Africa south of the Sahara.

The aardvark is a fairly common animal, but, being nocturnal and secretive, it is seldom seen in the wild. Often the only indications of the presence of aardvarks in an area are their burrows, scrape marks on termite hills, and the distinctive trails left by their tails as they drag along the ground. For a long time naturalists believed that they inhabited only savanna regions, but in 1906 aardvarks were discovered in the rain forests of Cameroon and Zaire. Because they dig burrows, they avoid swampy areas and very hard, stony places. Aardvarks can swim well, and one was seen swimming across 65 ft (20 m) of fast-flowing water.

Unlike other burrowing animals, aardvarks travel long distances in search of food. As a result, there are three types of burrows. The simplest burrows are just temporary holes dug while searching for food or escaping from predators. Only a little more complex are the semipermanent resting burrows, which are scattered several miles apart throughout an aardvark's home territory. This type of burrow is normally about 10–13 ft (3–4 m) long, and at the far end is a sleeping chamber just large enough for the animal to turn around in.

The most complex burrow systems are the permanent refuge burrows, which are excavated and maintained with some care and used, among other purposes, for raising the young. Such a burrow system may be up to 43 ft (13 m) long; and, although there is commonly only one entrance, there may be two, three, or occasionally four or five openings. The tunnels are about 16 in (40 cm) in diameter, and those leading away from the entrances slope down steeply at an angle of about 45 degrees. The tunnels follow a zigzag course, and at each bend there is a short blind tunnel, the

E. & D. Hosking/NHPA

This young aardvark (above) *may seem defenseless, but looks are very deceiving. It can burrow into the ground with astonishing speed and, if need be, can fend off attackers with an armory of eighteen claws.*

Anthony Bannister/NHPA

The rocky outcrops of the African plains provide all a hyrax's daily needs: food and water in the form of plants; shade and sun; and escape tunnels that it can use in times of need (left).

purpose of which is not known. They may be used for storing soil from other tunnels, or they may be where soil is collected to block off existing tunnels. There is usually one nesting chamber, which contains no nesting material apart from loose soil.

When an aardvark is digging, it rests on its hind legs and tail and scrapes at the soil using its strong, sharp claws. As it digs, it pushes the soil under its body with its powerful forelegs and disperses the heap with its hind legs and muscular tail. As digging progresses, the earth collects in a hemispherical mound around the entrance to the burrow. How the animal breathes underground, during this very strenuous activity, is not clear. An aardvark digs at a prodigious speed. It can dig a yard of tunnel in anything from five to twenty minutes, depending on the soil type, and it is said that it can dig faster than a team of men with shovels—although the theory that aardvarks are impossible to dig out of their burrows has been disproved.

A PLACE OF REFUGE

Abandoned burrows are often taken over by other creatures. Warthogs, sometimes with their entire litters, often take over aardvark burrows, and it is thought that warthogs take up residence in some regions only if there are enough abandoned aardvark holes in existence. Other animals that have been found in aardvark burrows include porcupines, hedgehogs, jackals, hyenas, mongooses, rodents, snakes, and birds. A species of bat roosts in aardvark burrows during the day. In emergencies, such as during a bush fire, aardvark burrows can offer shelter to an even wider range of animals.

The aardvark's burrow is its refuge. Its main enemies, apart from humans, are hunting dogs, hyenas, pythons, leopards, and lions. Even

in S I G H T

SAVING WATER

Like many animals that live in dry conditions and consequently need to conserve water, hyraxes have kidneys that reabsorb the maximum possible amount of water from their urine, which thereby becomes extremely concentrated.

The urine also contains a high proportion of calcium carbonate, and as hyraxes are in the habit of urinating always in the same places, large, white deposits of the chemical often build up. Europeans as well as Africans have used these deposits for a variety of medicinal purposes.

DISTRIBUTION

Hyraxes live in Africa south of the Sahara. Some of the rock hyraxes are found as far north as Libya, Algeria, and even Lebanon. Bush hyraxes live mainly in eastern Africa, while tree hyraxes inhabit evergreen forests in Africa's tropical belt.

K E Y

BUSH HYRAX

TREE HYRAX

ROCK HYRAX

AARDVARK

warthogs prey on young aardvarks. Running off and digging itself into the ground is the aardvark's first line of defense, but if cornered it will lash out with its heavy tail and forefeet, or lie on its back and slash with its claws. Sometimes the entrances of burrows are stopped up with earth, possibly to keep predators out. If an aardvark is threatened inside its burrow, it tries to dig deeper at first, but eventually turns back toward the surface.

CONEY ISLANDS

In contrast to the specialized aardvark, hyraxes are highly adaptable creatures. Their geographical range covers most of Africa and parts of the Middle East and includes habitats ranging from forests and plains to mountains at altitudes of more than 10,000 ft (3,000 m). Tree hyraxes are confined to the forests of central and southern Africa, including the islands of Fernando Po and Pemba. They reach altitudes of up to 15,000 ft (4,500 m).

Rock hyraxes are best adapted to dry regions and are thus the most widespread. They are the "coneys" referred to in the Bible and are found in Syria, Sinai, and Israel, as well as in much of

FOCUS ON

THE SERENGETI KOPJES

At the end of the rainy season the Serengeti is a sea of waving green grass. Dotted around this sea are small islands of stone, called kopjes. This word means "peaks" in Afrikaans, and this is exactly what they are—peaks of granite sticking up from the basement rock that underlies the sediments that form the Serengeti plains. Slow erosion of the hard granite over millions of years has smoothed and shaped these peaks.

The environmental conditions that these kopjes generate, and hence the fauna and flora they support, are completely different from the surrounding grassland. Because rainwater collects in the rock fissures and heavy dew forms on the rocks and plants each night, water is more plentiful than in the surroundings and the vegetation is thick and luxuriant. This itself helps to keep the atmosphere around the kopje humid and provides a barrier to the fires that sweep through the surrounding dry grass. When the rains come and the plains are flooded, the kopjes become islands in an even truer sense, because they remain unaffected.

TEMPERATURE AND RAINFALL

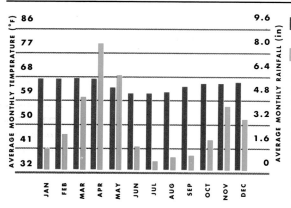

AVERAGE MONTHLY TEMPERATURE (°F): 86, 77, 68, 59, 50, 41, 32

AVERAGE MONTHLY RAINFALL (in): 9.6, 8.0, 6.4, 4.8, 3.2, 1.6, 0

JAN FEB MAR APR MAY JUN JUL AUG SEP OCT NOV DEC

■ TEMPERATURE

▨ RAINFALL

Lying so close to the equator, Tanzania experiences warmth all year round. The close passage of the sun in March causes a pressure drop, which results in heavy monsoon rains in April. There is a similar effect six months later.

Africa, particularly eastern Africa. They inhabit any rocky, scrubby area, in vegetation zones from arid to alpine where there is rocky shelter, or where they can dig burrows of their own. Bush hyraxes are restricted to northeastern and southern Africa. They, too, prefer to live among boulders and on rocky outcrops, but they are less well adapted for living in dry regions. In Africa the rocky outcrops that are found on the plains are called kopjes. They are like islands in a sea of grass, and they are usually inhabited by bush and rock hyraxes, which coexist happily because their food needs are quite different. The special "sticky" pads on the soles of their feet allow them to climb nimbly up the steepest and smoothest rock faces. ■

NEIGHBORS

The shady kopje plants shelter many animals. Antelope leap among the rocks, and birds of prey nest in the peaks. Baboons hunt lizards, and mongooses prey on hyraxes, rodents, and reptiles.

OLIVE BABOON

The olive baboon is an adaptable animal that includes both plant and animal matter in its diet.

EPAULETTED BAT

This fruit bat is common in eastern Africa, where it feeds on the fruits of savanna trees.

To the south of Lake Victoria, the Serengeti plains stretch over much of Tanzania. Here, rainfall is very seasonal and the most notable forms of wildlife are the huge migrating herds of grazing animals. Almost unnoticed, hyraxes live out their lives in and around the kopjes without having to move very far to find food.

SERENGETI PLAINS

Lake Victoria
KENYA
TANZANIA

ENEMIES

VERREAUX'S EAGLE
This is the hyrax's principal enemy. It nests in the crags of kopjes and is common wherever hyraxes abound.

MARTIAL EAGLE
This is the largest of the African eagles. It breeds in forests but hunts mammals and birds on the savanna.

ROCK PYTHON
When fully grown, this snake can kill a waterbuck. One individual was seen to swallow an impala.

EXTREMELY DANGEROUS

MODERATELY DANGEROUS

MODERATELY DANGEROUS

EGG-EATING SNAKE

This slim snake can swallow a whole chicken egg. It is not poisonous, but mimics other poisonous species.

LAPPET-FACED VULTURE

As Africa's largest vulture, this huge carrion-eater takes precedence over other vultures at carcasses.

RATEL

This ferocious nocturnal predator, also called the honey badger, often hides in aardvark burrows.

JACKSON'S CHAMELEON

This sinister-looking animal is actually harmless. Its only defense is its ability to change color very quickly.

SUNBIRD

The scarlet-crested sunbird has a long bill for sucking nectar from flowers, just like hummingbirds.

FOOD AND FEEDING

The aardvark appears to feed exclusively upon invertebrates. Although termites are its preferred food, when these are scarce it will eat other insects such as beetles, cockroaches, and grasshoppers, as well as their larvae. The aardvark also eats certain species of ants, although it avoids the large red ant and the ferocious African driver ant, both of which are capable of biting through even an aardvark's thick hide.

Termites, however, make up by far the largest part of the aardvark's diet. Any species will do, although the giant termite, being the largest, is clearly the best. The aardvark shares its habitats with other animals that feed on termites and ants. In the rain forests it competes with the giant pangolin, while on the savanna its fellow termite-eaters include the plains pangolin, the aardwolf, and the bat-eared fox.

NIGHT RAIDS

The aardvark is capable of daytime activity, but it prefers the cover of darkness. As it moves from place to place on its nightly foraging expeditions, it searches for large termite nests called termitaria. Where it can, it raids those of the giant termite, cracking open the packed, cementlike soil with its claws. As the mound is broken, termites scurry out onto the surface, and the aardvark scoops them up with its long, sticky tongue. Termites are not easy to digest, and part of the aardvark's large, saclike stomach acts like a gizzard: It is highly muscular and contains swallowed grit that helps grind up the tough skeletal shells of the insects.

During the night an aardvark may visit a number of nests, following a zigzag course from mound to mound. The route the animal follows changes every night and each nest may be left alone for five to eight days between raids. This gives the termites time to repair the nest and replenish their numbers. Recently repaired parts of a nest are usually soft, which makes the next raid much easier. Normally, a termite nest recovers quite easily from an aardvark attack, but occasionally the chamber that contains the queen and king is broken into, and this results in the death of the whole colony.

In between these mounded nests are underground nests of other savanna termite species, attracted there by the dry, trampled grass, which they use for nest-building, and the dry animal dung that is their source of food. These termites nest just below the surface and can quickly and easily be dug up by an aardvark.

in SIGHT

TERMITE DEFENSES

The giant termites' first line of defense is the sheer strength of their fortresslike mounds. These are constructed from a cementlike material, formed from termite feces mixed with soil and vegetation, that requires a pickax or hammer to break. In some cases mounds have defied the efforts of bulldozers to remove them, and people have had to resort to using explosives when trying to level termite-inhabited ground for development.

Termite soldiers have either strong jaws or long snouts that squirt a toxic, sticky liquid. But these weapons are not really intended for use against mammalian predators: They are used primarily against ants, with which termites are permanently at war.

BULLDOZED

Termitaria may be rockhard, but they are no match for the aardvark's slashing claws, and the insects' natural toxic defenses offer pitifully little resistance against the hardy mammal.

An aardvark demonstrates its digging prowess while searching for termites in Kenya.

David Keith Jones/Images of Africa

Aardvarks also feed on the columns of termites that emerge to forage for food at night; these are an essential part of the diet, as an aardvark could not possibly survive solely on the termites it can dig up. Some species swarm at night in broad columns 30–130 ft (10–40 m) long. For an aardvark such a column is a real find, because it can scoop up its prey with the minimum of effort, consuming less energy than when breaking open nests.

An aardvark has an acute sense of smell and very sensitive hearing, both of which it uses to trace termites. When searching for underground nests, an aardvark holds its snout near the ground, takes a few deep breaths, and then presses its nose firmly against the soil in order to sniff. It is not yet known, however, whether this method is used to detect scent or to trace the footfalls of thousands of tiny feet.

Unlike other ungulates, the aardvark buries its droppings in the soil excavated from its burrows. It does this by digging a hole some 4 in (10 cm) deep, defecating, and then refilling the hole with earth. The reason aardvarks evolved this habit is not clear, but it certainly benefits one particular plant, a species of gourd known in South Africa as the aardvark cucumber. The fruits of this plant are 2–4 in (5–9 cm) long and, unusual for gourds, develop underground. The aardvark eats this fruit to obtain the water inside, and the plant benefits by having its seeds carefully buried with the aardvark's dung, thus ensuring that they are dispersed and that they are provided with a source of food when they germinate. The plant also has a method of insuring that only those seeds that have passed through an aardvark's digestive system have a good chance of germination. Partial digestion probably weakens the outer coat and allows water to enter the seed much more easily. Those that remain uneaten do not normally germinate.

THE HYRAX DIET

Hyraxes are plant-eaters. They feed on a wide variety of plants, but rock hyraxes feed mainly on grass, while bush hyraxes browse mostly on the leaves of shrubs and trees. As a result, for most of the year these two kinds of hyraxes can live alongside one another without competing for resources. During the dry season, when grass becomes scarce, rock hyraxes turn to eating more of the leaves of shrubs, which starts to compete with the bush hyraxes. However, this does not appear to create problems except under very dry conditions, and it has been observed that rock and bush hyraxes do not occur together in very arid places.

Illustration Evi Antoniou

Tree hyraxes also feed on the leaves, shoots, and buds of trees, but they occupy rain forest habitats and so do not compete for food with bush hyraxes. Tree hyraxes include insects in their diet, as, indeed, rock hyraxes do: The Cape hyrax is said to be partial to locusts.

Most grazing and browsing ungulates crop grass or leaves with their incisor teeth. The incisors of hyraxes, however, are tusklike and are used for tearing bark off trees and eating succulent plants; they are razor-sharp and are more useful as defense weapons than for feeding. The hyrax has a somewhat inefficient method of eating grass. The head is turned to one side and the grass is pulled into the mouth using the tongue. Then the mouth is closed and the grass is torn away by the sharp-edged, high-crowned cheek teeth.

Hyraxes do not ruminate (regurgitate and redigest food), even though they perform jaw actions that give the appearance of chewing cud. However, they seem to digest tough plant material just as efficiently as ruminants. To do this, they have a complex gut arrangement with a large stomach and two separate appendixes. Bacterial digestion of cellulose takes place in the stomach and the first appendix; the purpose of the second, two-horned appendix is not yet clear.

In order to feed on grasses, rock hyraxes move away from the security of the kopje on to the surrounding plain, and, being vulnerable animals,

they have to feed somewhat cautiously. On a sunny day there are usually two distinct feeding periods. The first is in the morning—after they have warmed up and completed their morning grooming session—and lasts for up to three hours. During the hottest part of the day they return to the kopje to rest, coming out to feed again in the late afternoon and evening. Because hyraxes need to warm themselves in the sun before they can be very active, they do not emerge from the dens in poor weather. However, this is not usually a problem, since they are capable of fasting for a day.

An individual hyrax takes about 20 minutes to consume enough vegetation for a meal. As rock hyraxes feed, they divide into small groups, each of which forms a separate defensive unit. They form

BUSH TUCKER

Equipped with low-crowned teeth, bush hyraxes (below right) consume softer plant matter, including tender young shoots and berries.

ROUGH DIET

Rock hyraxes (below) feed mainly on coarse grasses, using their high-crowned molars to crush the roughage.

DINING ALOFT

Tree hyraxes (right) have the best of both worlds, since some species forage both in the branches and on the ground. Like the bush hyraxes, they feed on softer plant matter and, from time to time, a few insects.

a circle, facing out as they graze, so that the group has a clear view in all directions. At the first hint of danger the group heads for cover. Normally hyraxes do not stray more than 150 ft (45 m) from the kopje, but if the grazing becomes exhausted within this area, they have to venture farther out. To minimize the risks, they follow well-marked, familiar paths to such feeding areas.

Bush hyraxes can generally find their food on or very close to the kopje. They feed during the day on a wide variety of shrubs, including myrrh and hibiscus, but they are especially fond of acacia leaves and climb to the uppermost branches to find the tender shoots. In truth, hyraxes are highly adaptable and will eat almost any vegetation, if the situation demands. In the Karoo, in South Africa, the hyraxes' tendency to raid crops has made them enemies of the local farmers. ■

Eating is an inefficient business for a hyrax. With only a pair of short tusks for incisor teeth, the hyrax instead rips vegetation free with its tongue and palate (right).

Stephen Dalton/NHPA

Illustrations Steve Roberts/Wildlife Art Agency

SOCIAL STRUCTURE

Hyraxes live in colonies. Usually, all the members of a colony feed and sleep together, and on nice days lie together in dense groups on ledges to absorb the sun's warmth. At other times they like to play together among the rocks.

The company of others is important to them for two reasons. As with many other herbivores, living in a group provides a form of protection against predators: At any given time some individuals can be on sentry duty, while others sleep or feed. But hyraxes are not defenseless, and if a predator gets too close a hyrax will often show great bravery. It will turn to threaten its enemy with a fearsome display of bared teeth and snarling.

Sociable behavior also helps keep hyraxes warm. Their slow metabolism and poor temperature control oblige them to snuggle together, particularly on cold days; the young are especially vulnerable to heat loss. Hyraxes do not, however, indulge in social grooming. Each animal grooms its own fur, using its comblike lower incisor teeth and the long claw on the inner toe of each hind foot.

> WHEN A SENTRY GIVES A WARNING CRY, ALL THE OTHER HYRAXES ARE ALERTED; IF THE WARNING IS REPEATED MORE LOUDLY, THEY BOLT FOR COVER

A bush hyrax colony may contain up to about 35 individuals; rock hyraxes form smaller colonies of around 25. Within a colony hyraxes live in stable family groups, each of which usually contains from 3 to 7 related adult females, although in one group 17 were noted. The group is led by a mature territorial male, but there are also a few younger males, most of which will eventually disperse. There are also a number of juveniles of both sexes.

The family holds a territory that is handed down from one generation to the next, but its borders are not defended, and on large kopjes family ranges may overlap; occasionally, females may move from one family unit to the next. At the core of the territory, however, is an area that contains key resources, such as food, sunning ledges, and caves, and this area is defended by the lead male.

Young males that become too much of a threat are chased out of the group by the senior male. On small kopjes they do not survive for long, but on

A family group of yellow-spotted hyraxes enjoys the sunshine, young and old jostling together.

B. B. Murray/Oxford Scientific Films

in SIGHT

THE LONE AARDVARK

The aardvark spends nearly all of its time on its own. When two or more aardvarks are seen together, the likelihood is that they are a mother and her offspring. If a male meets a female in season, he may stay with her for a short time, during which they may forage as a pair. However, male aardvarks seem to spend virtually no time looking for or courting females, and it is assumed that they mate with any female they meet that happens to be in season.

Illustration Mark Stewart/Wildlife Art Agency

ON THE ROCKS

Prime living space is often at a premium, and rock hyrax family groups guard their core area with gusto, bristling and snarling at intruders (above).

larger outcrops they occupy the outlying areas. Among these peripheral males there is an established hierarchy, and if a territorial male is killed by a predator or dies naturally there is always another male ready to take its place.

Young males, and sometimes young females, often emigrate from the colony, generally traveling more than a mile (2 km) from their place of birth. Some wander off at 16–24 months old, others leave a little later, but in any case they do so before they are 30 months old. Emigration gives them the chance to colonize new areas or in some cases find a sexual partner in a different kopje. This helps to overcome the inbreeding, which inevitably occurs in small, tight-knit, static communities. ∎

REPRODUCTION

Animals that live in habitats where the climate varies a lot through the year often time their breeding so that births coincide with the season in which food is abundant. Female hyraxes breed once a year, and the birth rate peaks during the rainy season, when they all give birth within three weeks of one another. Female bush hyraxes produce between one and three offspring in each litter, while rock hyraxes produce up to four. When an adult female comes into season, she remains receptive for several days. Gestation lasts about seven months, and when the young are born they are well developed: They can walk around and jump.

Most species of hyraxes have four teats in the groin and two more near the shoulders. Soon after birth, young hyraxes establish a strict teat regime in which each individual is assigned its own particular teats—the number of teats assigned to each one depends, of course, upon the size of the litter. The young are weaned at one to five months. Both sexes become sexually mature at 16–17 months, and at this stage females become part of the adult

BREEDING

Bush hyraxes usually breed once a year, the birth rate peaking during the rainy season, when food is most abundant.

(in) SIGHT

INTERBREEDING

In spite of the fact that rock and bush hyraxes associate very closely with each other, they do not interbreed. Several factors may account for this. The territorial calls of male rock hyraxes are different from those of bush hyraxes, and this in itself may serve to keep the species apart during the breeding season.

In addition, the behavior of a male rock hyrax prior to copulation is different from that of a bush hyrax. However, there is also a physical barrier to interbreeding: The anatomy of the male sex organs is different. The penis of a male rock hyrax is short, simple, and elliptical in crosssection, while the penis of a bush hyrax is long and uniquely structured.

Illustration Darren Morrell/Wildlife Art Agency

Like many hoofed mammals, hyrax youngsters are well developed at birth and grow rapidly (above).

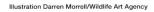

Bob Campbell/Survival Anglia

group. Males remain with the group for a time, but disperse before they reach the age of 30 months.

Although the proportion of males to females at birth is equal, adult females live longer than males, which is why there are invariably fewer males than females in a colony; in some species there may be half as many. The most likely reason for the higher survival rate of females is that they are always part of tight-knit groups, which are less vulnerable to attack than males, who tend to forage alone and often try to travel between groups.

Very little is known about the aardvark's reproductive habits in the wild. A female in heat is visited by several males—one of the rare occasions when adult aardvarks are seen together. Gestation takes about seven months and young aardvarks are probably born at the start of the rainy season, when the supply of termites increases. In Zaire aardvarks are born in October or November, while in Ethiopia most are born in May or June.

Each female usually bears just one offspring at a time, occasionally two. The newborn aardvark is naked, has limp ears and wrinkled, tender skin, and weighs about 4 lb (2 kg). Within hours of being born it tries to walk and seek out its mother's teats. It stays in the nest burrow until it is about two

FROM BIRTH TO DEATH

ROCK HYRAX

GESTATION: 210–240 DAYS	**WEANING:** 3–6 MONTHS
NUMBER OF LITTERS PER YEAR: 1, DURING RAINY SEASON	**SEXUAL MATURITY:** 16–18 MONTHS
LITTER SIZE: 1–4	**LONGEVITY:** 9–14 YEARS

weeks old, at which time it starts to accompany its mother on foraging expeditions. At three weeks old it starts to eat termites.

Over the next few months the pair occupies a series of burrows—the mother digs a new one about every eight days—and at six months the youngster starts to dig its own burrows. However, it remains near its mother and forages with her until at least the start of the next mating season. If the young is male, it leaves its mother at this time, but females often stay with their mothers for longer, and it is therefore quite common to see a female with two young of different ages. By the time an aardvark is a year old, it is almost as large as an adult. However, it probably does not reach sexual maturity until it is over two years old. It is not known how long aardvarks live in the wild, but captive specimens have lived for up to ten years. ■

SUCKLING
Female hyraxes have a pair of teats at the shoulders (left) *as well as teats located in the groin.*

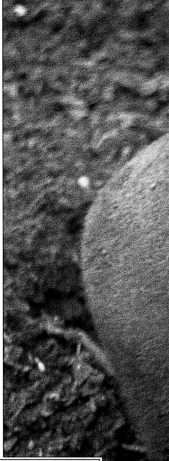

Unseen and Untroubled

ALTHOUGH FEW PEOPLE EVER GET TO SEE AN AARDVARK, ITS PLENTIFUL BURROWS TESTIFY TO ITS CONTINUING SUCCESS AS A SPECIES. THE HYRAXES, TOO, ARE GENERALLY THRIVING

The aardvark is not currently regarded as being endangered. However, it is a fairly well protected species, since by law it cannot be hunted in many countries. A substantial number of aardvarks are in national parks and reserves, particularly in East and South Africa.

Nevertheless, aardvarks are not common, largely because they live only where giant termites can be found and avoid rocky places, hard soils, and damp sites where their burrows might flood. Being shy, they are rarely seen in the wild, so their populations are not easy to assess by observation. However, the evidence of their burrows is only too obvious, and seems to indicate that, where they do exist, their numbers are being maintained at a reasonable level.

HUNTING

As with many other species, however, the status of the aardvark requires regular monitoring, for various reasons. To begin with, it has for centuries been hunted by humans. It is prized as a source of food, and said by some people to "look like beef but taste like pork," although others say that it is as tough as leather and smells very strong. Its teeth are used by several tribes in Zaire to make charms. Its bristly hair is sometimes ground up and is said to be a powerful poison when added to the local beer, although there is little evidence that this is so. Its skin is sometimes made into leather straps. Where flying termites are gathered by humans for food, natives put aardvark claws into their collecting baskets in the belief that this will increase their harvest.

A FARMING PEST

Aardvarks share their habitats with humans—the soft soil that they prefer to dig in is also prized by farmers for growing crops, and grassy plains are useful for raising cattle. And because aardvarks have a very limited diet, they are vulnerable to changes in their habitat that affect the supply of termites. Thus intensive crop production, which disturbs the soil, discourages both termites and aardvarks. In addition, aardvark burrows are often regarded as a nuisance by farmers, who try to eradicate them from their land. Paradoxically, this can lead to a rapid increase in the local population of termites, which themselves can become a problem.

On the other hand, the herding cattle, which trample the grass and create better conditions for termites, may actually boost aardvark numbers.

F. Hartmann/Frank Lane Picture Agency

The expansion of crop farming in Africa has reduced the aardvark's habitat (above).

Pat Morris/Ardea

This map shows the current distribution of the eastern tree hyrax.

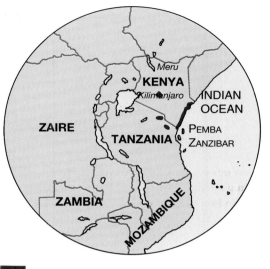

■ **EASTERN TREE HYRAX**

Of all the hyraxes, the eastern tree hyrax is currently believed to be the most endangered, largely as a result of hunting for its fur and flesh. It is found today in Kilimanjaro, Meru, Usambara, Pemba, Zanzibar, and the coast of Kenya. There is concern for all the tree hyraxes, since their rain-forest home is under attack and they may not be able to adapt to other habitats.

But until more is known about aardvark behavior and ecology, little can be done to assess scientifically the risks or benefits created by agriculture or to devise any sort of population management plan.

HOPE FOR HYRAXES

As far as is known, none of the various species of rock and bush hyraxes are at risk. They are lucky in that their kopje habitats are largely well protected in parks and reserves, and in any case are not used by humans for any purpose. Although some natives regard hyraxes as good to eat, most species are not extensively hunted for either their flesh or their fur. They are under constant attack by predators, such as the cobra and puff adder, eagles, owls and buzzards, hunting dogs, big cats, and mongooses. On top of this their reproductive rate is low compared to similar mammals; however, they still manage to sustain their numbers.

Zoologists have gained most of their knowledge of the shy aardvark from studying it in captivity.

The factor most likely to trouble bush and rock hyraxes would be a dramatic change in climate. Excessive heat and drought, always a possibility in Africa, would result in a scarcity of food, and because of the difficulty they have in maintaining their body temperature, hyraxes would not survive very long if the climate cooled. Historically, they have never managed to disperse far out of Africa, and today competition with humans and other animal species would almost certainly preclude them from doing so. Their survival, therefore, depends on the preservation of their present habitats, which fortunately are not currently under threat.

Tree hyraxes, on the other hand, do appear to have some problems. The ancestors of these animals must have been highly adaptable: In order to gain a foothold in the niche they now occupy, they had to lose their dependence on rocks for shelter, improve their temperature control, and become more adept at climbing trees, as well as become

HYRAXES IN DANGER

THIS IS HOW THE INTERNATIONAL UNION FOR THE CONSERVATION OF NATURE (IUCN) CURRENTLY CLASSIFIES THE HYRAX AND AARDVARK:

EASTERN TREE HYRAX	INDETERMINATE

INDETERMINATE MEANS THAT THE SPECIES MAY BE THREATENED TO SOME DEGREE, BUT THERE IS TOO LITTLE INFORMATION FOR A MORE PRECISE RATING. THE AARDVARK WAS FORMERLY LISTED IN APPENDIX 2 OF CITES, WHICH PROVIDES LEGAL PROTECTION, BUT WAS DOWNLISTED IN 1992.

nocturnal rather than diurnal. By achieving all these things they managed to compete with the rain-forest rodents and primates.

It is ironic, therefore, that, having achieved all this, tree hyraxes are now, like most rain-forest animals, under threat due to the removal of their habitat by deforestation. As yet, no hyrax species are regarded as endangered, although the eastern tree hyrax is listed by the International Union for the Conservation of Nature (see above). This species has been singled out for particular attention because it is widely hunted by local people in the forests around Mount Kilimanjaro, Tanzania, for its soft, dense fur, as well as for its flesh. The fur is made into rugs; it is said that 48 animals are needed in order to produce just one rug. ∎

ALONGSIDE MAN

BIBLICAL CONEYS

In the Bible, Solomon is reported to have said, "The coney . . . a weak race, yet it places its home among the rocks." He was quite correct, of course, but since *coney* was an old English word for "rabbit," no one realized that he was, in fact, referring to hyraxes!

The error occurred in translation. The original Hebrew text uses the word *shaphan*, which was translated by Martin Luther into the German word for "rabbit," and later translated into the English word *coney*. Luther, being unfamiliar with hyraxes, thought that Solomon was referring to rabbits; this error is perpetuated in Bibles today.

Luther was not the only one to be confused by these animals. When, about 3,000 years ago, Phoenician sailors reached the western Mediterranean, they found a land inhabited by rabbit-sized animals that looked like hyraxes. They therefore named it *Ishaphan*, "the land of the hyraxes," a name later changed by the Romans to *Hispania*, from which the modern names España and Spain are derived. But the Phoenicians were wrong: Hyraxes have never existed in this part of the Mediterranean, and the animals they saw were, of course, rabbits!

Tree hyraxes evolved to be able to exploit the rich food supplies in the canopy of the rainforest.

John Shaw/NHPA

INTO THE FUTURE

Aardvarks are adaptable and easy to keep in zoos. The first captive aardvark was taken to London Zoo in 1869, and it and its successors appeared to have settled in quite happily. In captivity they are mostly nocturnal, as one would expect, but zoo specimens do wake up during the day; they even sunbathe. This is easier to do in a temperate climate than in the hot sun of their native land, and it suggests that in such conditions they feel more secure. Even their feeding habits are adaptable. Although they are primarily termite-eaters, in zoos they adapt to a diet of chopped meat, eggs, oatmeal, and milk, with added vitamins and formic acid.

Aardvarks have also been bred in zoos. However, breeding programs have not been all that successful. The first zoo-bred aardvarks were born in Frankfurt Zoo in Germany in 1962, but they and subsequent young born at this zoo died.

Illustration Kim Thompson

PREDICTION

CONTINUING SUCCESS
Natural predators will continue to take their toll, but the aardvark and hyraxes have healthy populations and are under no imminent threats. There is, however, some concern over the tree hyraxes: Their future depends on the preservation of their forest home.

In Amsterdam one female reared a young aardvark by herself, although it, too, died at six months. More recently, however, several aardvarks have been successfully raised by hand in Miami, Florida.

Hyraxes are even easier to keep in captivity. They are easy to feed and quickly become tame, although if they are handled roughly they defend themselves aggressively. Unlike the aardvark, captive hyraxes breed readily. If aardvarks and hyraxes were to become endangered in the wild, there is, therefore, every chance that zoos would be able to sustain them. This begs the question, however, of whether or not keeping such captive "specimens" is really worthwhile. If a species is extinct in the wild, is there any real justification for trying to keep it going in captivity? There are instances of zoo-bred animals being released into the wild—the Arabian oryx is a good example. Luckily, this is not yet necessary for either hyraxes or the aardvark. ■

AFRICAN FORESTS

The tropical rain forests of Africa are, as in other parts of the world, being exploited for their timber. The chances of halting this process are remote, so the logical solution is to find a way of exploiting the forests on a sustainable basis.

Selective logging is often promoted as a safe option, but studies have shown that removing just 18 percent of the trees can destroy 50 percent of the canopy. This is very bad news for those animals, such as tree hyraxes, that rely on unbroken canopy.

Alternatively, pressure can be taken off the remaining forest by planting new timber on land where the forest has been stripped. These forests must be mixed. Softwoods are useful because they grow quickly, but the demand for hardwoods is such that, even though they take much longer to grow, they too must be planted.

CARRIERS OF DISEASE

Hyraxes, like several other animal species, especially among the dog family, are affected by the human disease leishmaniasis. This disease is caused by a single-celled parasite and is transferred from one host to another by biting sandflies. The disease is treated by injecting the patient with drugs containing antimony, and without such treatment the disease can be fatal. As yet, no effective form of immunization has been discovered, and the best way of preventing it is to destroy diseased animals and spray against sandflies. Unfortunately, studies in Kenya and Ethiopia have indicated that hyraxes may be an important reservoir of this disease. What, if anything, will be done about this has yet to be seen.

ANTEATERS

28

François Gohier/Ardea

Anteaters belong to a small order of mammals called Edentata. Other edentates in this order are sloths and armadillos. All are toothless and live in Central or South America. Pangolins are also edentates, but they belong to a separate order and live in Africa and Asia.

ORDER

Edentata
(edentates)

FAMILY

Myrmecophagidae
(anteaters)

THREE GENERA

FOUR SPECIES

Myrmecophaga tridactyla
(giant anteater)

Cyclopes tetradactyla
(silky anteater)

Tamandua mexicana
(northern tamandua)

Tamandua tetradactyla
(southern tamandua)

TOOTHLESS WONDERS

EVOLVED OVER SIXTY MILLION YEARS, THE PRESENT-DAY ANTEATER, WITH ITS ELONGATED HEAD; TUBULAR, TOOTHLESS MUZZLE; AND LONG, SHARP CLAWS, IS CUSTOM-MADE TO SEARCH FOR ITS FAVORITE FOOD

s day breaks on a remote savanna grassland in northern South America, one of the world's most peculiar mammals emerges from its resting place beneath a bush to feed. Its body, which is about the size of a wolf's but flattened from side to side like a cardboard cutout, is clothed in coarse shaggy hair.

Its tail, too, is covered with long hairs trailing down to the ground, so that it resembles a living flag. This bizarre creature ambles along with an awkward limping gait, moving on its knuckles, with its huge powerful front claws folded inward. It leads a largely solitary life, spending much of each day in a methodical search for its specialized diet of ants and termites.

TRUE ANTEATERS

The giant anteater is the largest of the four species of true anteaters, all of which live in Central and

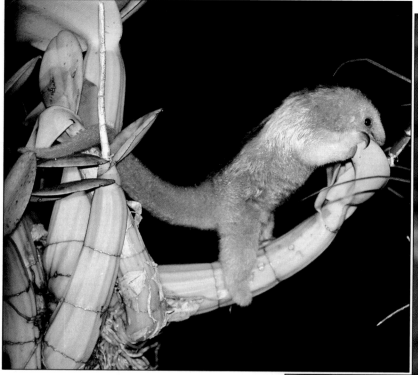

Carol Farneti/Planet Earth Pictures

Alan Root/Survival Anglia

Because of its nocturnal habits, the tiny silky anteater is seen more rarely than its larger relatives.

A tamandua and baby. Unlike giant anteaters, young tamanduas do not resemble their parents.

South America. It is the only one that can be found in open grasslands, though it occurs in a variety of other habitats, too, from semiarid regions to swamps and rain forests. The other anteater species—the two species of tamandua and the silky anteater—are restricted to forests.

STRANGE RELATIVES

The four anteaters are members of a small group of strange mammals, the edentates, which are classified together within the order Edentata

PRIMITIVE TRAITS, SUCH AS FIVE TOES ON THE HIND FEET, A SIMPLE UTERUS, AND A SMALL UNCOMPLICATED BRAIN, LINK ANTEATERS TO THE EARLIEST MAMMALS

(eed-en-tah-ta). The name means "without teeth," although in fact only the anteaters are entirely toothless. The other edentates, the tree sloths and armadillos, do have teeth, though these are generally hardly impressive, being reduced to a few rudimentary peglike structures, except for the enlarged caninelike premolars of the sloths.

As well as the fast-moving, armor-suited

armadillos and the proverbially slow-moving, tree-dwelling sloths, the edentates include a variety of equally odd, extinct groups. These include three families of giant ground sloths, some of which stood up to 6 ft (1.8 m) tall, and four families of tanklike *glyptodonts*, which resembled huge armadillos with massive, rigid body armor. One of these was as big as a small car and another defended itself against predators by flailing out at them with its great tail, which ended in a bony club armed with sharp spikes and looked like the mace carried by medieval knights.

THE *GLYPTODONT* WAS TOTALLY ENCASED IN SOLID ARMOR, WHICH MADE UP SOME 20 PERCENT OF ITS WEIGHT

In contrast to the anteaters, the *glyptodonts* were grazing animals. Although the fronts of their mouths were toothless, they were equipped with powerful teeth at the back for grinding up their diet of grasses and other vegetation. To power this battery of grinding teeth, they had strong muscles set in huge, deep jaws.

LIVING IN A NICHE

A few more species of mammals have evolved in other parts of the world to exploit the same diet as the "true" anteaters of the Americas. The pangolins of Africa and Asia were once called scaly anteaters and were grouped with the true anteaters, but they are now placed in an order of their own. Other ant-eating specialists are the aardvark of Africa; the numbat, or banded anteater, of Australia (*below*); and the echidnas, or spiny anteaters of Australia and New Guinea.

By about two million years ago, the armor plating of these strange animals had become fused to form a rigid, dome-shaped, bony shell consisting of a mosaic of polygonal plates.

The giant ground sloths looked totally unlike the present-day sloths of Central and South America, with big bearlike heads. The biggest known, called *Megatherium*, probably weighed as much as three tons (three tonnes) and was the size of an elephant.

These odd creatures ranged widely through North and South America until historical times and feature in the legends of the Araucan of Chile and Tehuelche Indians of Patagonia.

MYSTERIOUS BEGINNINGS

The origin of the edentates—and their relationships with other mammals—is shrouded in mystery. Zoologists are divided on whether they all evolved from a single ancestor or evolved from several distinct groups. The fossil record of these fascinating animals is unfortunately poor; the earliest known anteaters, such as Protamandua, which lived about twenty million years ago, looked very much like their modern-day descendents.

Recently, an exciting find was made of a fossil anteater called Eutamandua, complete with the remains of fossilized ants. Its appearance—which indicated that it would have closely resembled today's tamanduas—was not very surprising. What was remarkable was where it was found: in oil shale deposits near Frankfurt, Germany. Until this discovery, scientists thought that anteaters had never existed outside tropical America. ■

ⒶNCESTORS

The anteaters and their relatives evolved about 60 million years ago in South America, which was separated from the North American continent by ocean. Then, about five million years ago, the land bridge that had briefly united North and South America was reestablished. Members of this strange group of animals, including massively armored *plyptodonts*, giant ground sloths, and armadillos, as well as a variety of anteaters, were able to travel across the bridge and colonize the north. Since then, the anteaters and sloths disappeared, probably unable to compete with more successful northern mammals.

NORTHERN TAMANDUA
Tamandua mexicana
(*tam-AND-oo-a MEKSI-kana*)

Tamanduas have a smoother coat of hair than their giant relative and a naked prehensile tail. All subspecies have a broad black line running along their backs and extending into a "collar" and "vest."

SOUTHERN TAMANDUA
Tamandua tetradactyla
(*tam-AND-oo-a tet-ra-DAK-tilla*)

Very similar to its northern cousin, but more variable in the pattern of its coat. Some subspecies are all gold, others all brown or all black, and yet others have a partial or entire "vest."

All illustrations Evi Antoniou

SILKY ANTEATER

Cyclopes tetradactyla

(*sy-CLO-peez tet-ra-DAK-tilla*)

The size of a squirrel. In the northern part of its range, it is a uniform gold color. Southern species are grayer with a dark stripe down the back.

The order Edentata (*eed-en-TAH-tah*), which anteaters share today with armadillos and sloths, contains an assortment of strange mammals that flourished in the New World between about 60 million and 2 million years ago. The earliest edentates, which appeared in North America and may have looked like mongooses with armadillolike heads, managed to reach South America before becoming extinct. There they radiated into many different species, divisible into three main groups: armored forms, represented today by armadillos; "hairy" forms, including the modern tree sloths; and the anteaters. Only a fraction of the diversity of this fascinating group of animals is alive today, and most are relatively little known.

GIANT ANTEATER

Myrmecophaga tridactyla

(*meer-MEKO-fay-ga try-DAK-tilla*)

The giant anteater is the only member of its family that is not largely tree-dwelling. Although perfectly capable of climbing trees when the occasion demands, it spends most of its life on the ground. Its habit of lying in a hollow to sleep with its great bushy tail wrapped around it like a blanket, combined with the protective striped pattern of its foreparts, helps it avoid detection by predators such as jaguars and pumas.

OTHER EDENTATES AND PHOLIDOTA

(*Sloths, armadillos, and pangolins*)

33

ANATOMY:
THE
GIANT ANTEATER

The giant anteater's shoulder height is about 2 ft (60 cm), and it weighs about 77 lb (35 kg). Its smallest relative, the silky anteater, by contrast, is only about 16 in (40 cm) long, including its long tail, and weighs a mere 10–18 oz (300–500 g).

THE SNOUT

The giant anteater's snout is long and tube shaped and ends in a tiny mouth opening. It contains the long, cylindrical nose; the anteater has an acute sense of smell, which is probably about 40 times more sensitive than a human's.

TONGUE

The tongue is worm-shaped and about 2 ft (60 cm) long. Huge glands beneath it keep the tongue coated with saliva, which enables the anteater to flick it in and out of its mouth at a rate of up to 150 times a minute and trap ants and termites on the sticky coating.

Anatomy illustrations William Oliver/Wildlife Art Agency

X RAY

ANTEATER SKELETON

The giant anteater's skeleton is very elongated, with forelimbs adapted for breaking into ants' and termites' nests and for defense against predators. It also has expanded ribs, which help the animal maximize the striking force it can deliver when standing on its hind legs and slashing with its front claws at an enemy.

VERTEBRA OF GIANT ANTEATER

Unlike other mammals, anteaters and their relativ have extra jointlike projections on the rear vertebrae of their backs, making their lower backb unusually rigid and able t cope with tearing into an nests and standing erect v defending themselves.

X-ray illustrations Elisabeth Smith

GIANT ANTEATER

The front feet bear two extremely long claws, that of the third digit being 4 in (10 cm) long. When walking, the anteater tucks in these giant claws, moving on its knuckles and the sides of its forefeet.

TAMANDUA

In both species of tamanduas the three middle digits bear the sharp claws that they use to tear apart ants' and termites' nests.

SILKY ANTEATER

The first, fourth, and fifth digits of the silky anteater are much reduced. A long third digit extending into a fleshy pad, stiffened by a bone, acts as a "thumb" to aid grasping.

TAIL

The enormous, bushy tail measures 2–3 ft (65–90 cm) long and is covered in hairs up to 16 in (40 cm) long. It is held erect, like a flag, continuing the line of the mane along the anteater's back. When resting the anteater wraps its tail around itself, like a blanket.

HIND FEET

The anteater's hind feet have five toes of more or less equal length. It plants the soles of its feet firmly on the ground when it walks, like a bear or a human.

GIANT ANTEATER SKULL

The giant anteater has the most modified skull, almost tubular in shape. Like those of other anteaters, its jaws are completely toothless. The skull lacks the strong projections found in other mammals for the attachment of chewing muscles, and the tongue-retracting muscles are anchored to the animal's breastbone.

TAMANDUA SKULL

The tamandua has a much shorter snout than its larger relatives, with an even smaller opening for the mouth—it is only the diameter of a pencil.

SILKY ANTEATER SKULL

The silky anteater has a short, pointed, curved snout, with a much larger mouth opening than that found in its relatives.

SOLITARY WANDERERS

DESPITE THE ABUNDANCE OF INSECT PREY, THE ANTEATER SPENDS MOST OF ITS WAKING HOURS ON THE MOVE, SEARCHING FOR AN EASY MEAL

Evolution has equipped the anteater to do two things superbly well: eat and sleep. A giant anteater may spend up to 15 hours a day asleep, usually in a shallow depression, which it digs in the shade of a bush. Covered by its great plume of a tail and disguised by its strawlike hair and cryptic patterning, it lies virtually invisible among the dry grasses of the broad South American plains.

Yet it is not entirely unconscious. Its keen sense of hearing is always active, and the slightest sound in the vicinity will alert it to a potential threat such as a jaguar or an inquisitive human. Rousing itself, the anteater extends its long, curved snout and sniffs the air in all directions. If all is well it settles down again, but if necessary it will take off at a

A GIANT ANTEATER CAN USE THE PRODIGIOUS STRENGTH OF ITS FORELIMBS TO CRUSH AN ADVERSARY TO DEATH

clumsy gallop to find a safer refuge, or even rear up to defend itself. A giant anteater can disembowel a dog with a single slash of its claws. Toothless it may be, but a giant anteater is no easy target.

The giant anteater moves quite rapidly over the ground despite its awkward gait: the highly developed claws force it to walk on the outer edges of its "hands" with the claws folded inward. The tamanduas are even clumsier, stumbling stiff-legged through the grass, but, supported by their tails, they can effectively climb in the trees. The silky anteater is strictly arboreal, using its mobile prehensile tail and highly modified hind feet to grip stems while it probes for prey with its hands.

In general, anteaters are most active at night. The tree-dwelling silky anteater is exclusively nocturnal, and has been seen foraging in daylight

only when disoriented by capture and sedation. The ground-dwelling giant anteater will feed by day in areas where it feels secure, but near areas of human habitation it, too, prefers to forage at night. The two species of tamanduas are primarily nocturnal, usually spending their days asleep in tree hollows, but they are occasionally seen in daylight, both on the ground and in the trees. As species and as individuals, tamanduas are more

A giant anteater sleeps in the shade of a tree (right). Its bushy tail provides effective camouflage.

J.M. Austerman/Oxford Scientific Films

The giant anteater (above) is instantly recognizable by its long snout and clumsy gait.

Adrian Warren/Ardea

Alan Root/Survival Anglia

When threatened, the apparently clumsy tamandua (above) *rears up in a fierce display of power.*

flexible in their behavior and will vary their patterns to exploit feeding opportunities that arise.

This flexibility may be important to the survival of all four species, because it minimizes the competition between them. Where giant anteaters

ONCE THEY ARE AWAKE, ALL ANTEATERS FORAGE OVER EXTENSIVE AREAS THAT ARE RELATIVE TO THEIR SIZE

are scarce on the ground, the local tamanduas may feed extensively on ground-dwelling ants, leaving those in the trees to be exploited by the silky anteater population. But where giant anteaters are common, there is less scope for foraging on the ground, and the tamanduas tend to be more arboreal. Since a tamandua weighs some 20 times as much as a silky anteater, it is restricted to the thicker, more sturdy branches, while the smaller species can forage in the twigs of the treetops.

These factors insure that each anteater species occupies its own niche in the ecosystem. Obviously any animal will feed where and when it can, regardless of others, but over time a species with a reliable food supply will do better than a similar species that has to compete with others.

Thus, natural selection has favored a division of the spoils between the anteaters, with the largest and smallest species adhering to their own, very different habits, and the two intermediate species—which never coexist—acquiring the flexibility to make the most of their opportunities. ■

HABITATS

The true anteaters are restricted to tropical Central and South America, from southern Mexico to northern Argentina. This area encompasses a wide variety of habitats, from steamy rain forest to semiarid grassland, and the four anteater species have evolved to exploit them all.

OPEN-COUNTRY SPECIALIST

The giant anteater is an open-country specialist. Too heavy and clumsy to feed in the trees, it raids the earthen fortresses of large ground-nesting ants, such as the carpenter ants of the Venezuelan llanos, striding purposefully through the stiff grass with its long snout held just above the ground to detect the slightest trace of prey. When it is not foraging it curls up in a hollow in the ground, relying on the long grass for cover. Even where there is dense vegetation nearby, it rarely takes advantage of the security it might offer.

THE ANTEATER'S SIZE, POWER, AND CAN-OPENER CLAWS GIVE IT THE CONFIDENCE TO FACE ANY PREDATOR

The giant anteater's willingness to forage over large areas enables it to flourish in dry, virtually treeless regions where ant colonies are fairly thinly distributed, but it is most numerous in lush grassland and open tropical forest. In such areas it shares its habitat with the smaller, more arboreal tamandua.

BORDERLINE SPECIES

The two species of tamandua are found throughout the range of anteaters as a whole, with the northern tamandua occurring from Mexico to western Colombia and the southern tamandua from this point south throughout the Amazon Basin. The boundary between their distributions is sharply defined along a line west of the Andes, and the two are rarely found together. In the area near the boundary, the southern tamandua is distinguished from the northern by its lack of a black "vest" pattern; but farther south the pattern reappears on the southern, and individuals found in the far south look a lot like the northern species. For this reason the two were originally regarded as the same species with many local races; there are at least eighteen races recognized today.

Regardless of species or race, however, the habits of tamanduas are much the same from Mexico to Bolivia. Clumsy and awkward on the

Francois Gohier/Ardea

DISTRIBUTION

GIANT ANTEATER

TAMANDUA

SILKY TWO-TOED ANTEATER

The silky anteater has a wide distribution from southern Mexico through to the Amazon Basin, but it is found only in dense forest. The giant anteater occurs in both open forest and treeless grassland, from Guatemala to northern Paraguay and Argentina. The two species of tamanduas are found in forested areas, with the northern species ranging from southern Mexico to western Colombia, and the southern species ranging from Colombia to Bolivia and Brazil.

● Anteaters are believed to be among the first animals to have colonized the continent of South America more than 60 million years ago.

● In prehistoric times the warm, humid South American forests had a great diversity of anteater species. Nearly all are now extinct: Only four distinct species remain.

● Anteaters have adapted to a wide range of habitats in equatorial and tropical regions and are found wherever there is a plentiful supply of the ants and other insects that make up their diet.

A giant anteater testing the air. It has no teeth, but a long, narrow tongue, which it uses to extract vast amounts of ants and termites from their mounds.

ground, they often prefer to forage among trees and thorn scrub, where they can put their muscular prehensile tails to good use. Being lighter, less well armed, and slower than the giant anteater, they are also more vulnerable on the ground, so they normally sleep in trees where they are relatively safe from jaguars and pumas.

Provided there are some trees in the vicinity, however, tamanduas will readily feed on ground-dwelling ants and termites. In the tropical forests of Barro Colorado Island, Panama, the northern

---

BOTH SPECIES OF TAMANDUAS ALTER THEIR HABITS TO SUIT THEIR HABITATS, AVAILABLE PREY, AND COMPETITION

---

tamandua spends roughly half its time feeding on the ground. In more open habitats it may spend longer, but nearly always retreats to the trees during the day. In densely forested regions of Venezuela, the southern tamandua may spend up to 70 percent of its time aloft, feeding mainly among the stronger lower branches of the forest trees. Competition can be a significant factor in open forest, where tamanduas and giant anteaters may forage on the ground for the same prey, but

The tamandua spends most of its time in trees; it uses its prehensile tail to assist in climbing.

in dense rain forest the competition between anteater species is reduced by the extra scope that the tree cover provides.

LAYERS OF LIFE

A tropical forest is a three-dimensional environment, like an ocean: Animals can live at all levels, spacing themselves vertically as well as horizontally, vastly increasing the potential number of animals per square mile. Because the nature of

---

THE SILKY ANTEATER FALLS PREY TO OWLS AND EAGLES, WHICH PLUCK IT FROM THE BRANCHES LIKE RIPE FRUIT

---

the habitat changes at each level, however, the nature of the resident animals changes, too. The forest floor, the understory, the thicker branches, and the slender twigs of the canopy all tend to support different species, each constrained by their respective diets, climbing skills, and weight.

In the case of anteaters, the diets of the four species are very similar, but their climbing skills and weights cover a broad spectrum. The giant anteater is restricted to the forest floor, but the

FOCUS ON

AMAZON RAIN FOREST

South America is covered by Amazon rain forests, which are mostly situated to the north of the continent. The hot and damp conditions there have created a habitat for a wealth of animal and plant life.

Because the tall, evergreen trees cast deep shade, many of the animals are found living high up in the tree canopy, where there is more light. Even plants grow mainly high in the trees. The branches teem with birds, monkeys, and tree-dwelling snakes and amphibians.

On the forest floor are deer and antelope and tree-climbing cats, and the area is home to innumerable species of insects, many of them found in vast numbers. These include the ants and termites on which the anteater feeds.

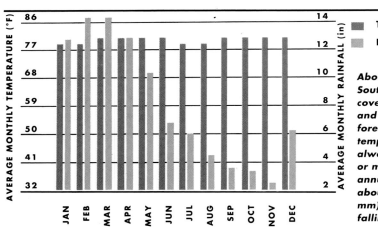

TEMPERATURE AND RAINFALL

Chart: AVERAGE MONTHLY TEMPERATURE (°F) — 86, 77, 68, 59, 50, 41, 32. AVERAGE MONTHLY RAINFALL (in) — 14, 12, 10, 8, 6, 4, 2. Months: JAN, FEB, MAR, APR, MAY, JUN, JUL, AUG, SEP, OCT, NOV, DEC.

■ TEMPERATURE
■ RAINFALL

About one-third of South America is covered by warm and humid rain forests. Here, temperatures are always 65°F (18.5°C) or more and the annual rainfall is about 80 in (2,032 mm), with some rain falling daily.

tamanduas can feed at any level where the branches are strong enough to support them. The very highest levels, however, are the preserve of the silky anteater, a squirrel-sized acrobat capable of foraging for prey among twigs and vines barely thick enough to carry the weight of a bird.

The silky anteater occurs throughout the tropical forests of Central and South America. It is probably the most numerous of the anteaters, yet, owing to its nocturnal habits and reluctance to descend to ground level, it is rarely seen. ∎

NEIGHBORS

The rain forest is home to more wildlife per square mile than any other habitat. This rich diversity includes some awesome predators.

KING VULTURE

This large bird of prey, with a bald but brightly colored head, is found in all the anteaters' territory.

EMERALD TREE BOA

This bright green rain forest snake hangs in coils on tree branches, uncoiling to drop on its prey.

All illustrations Kim Thompson

THE AMAZON BASIN

The area around the mouth of the Amazon, which lies across the equator, consists of grassy marshland. Toward its mouth the river is 18 mi (30 km) wide and inland it is 2–4 mi (3–6.5 km) wide, with many tributaries. It is surrounded by rain forest, home to a diversity of life.

ATLANTIC OCEAN

BRAZIL

JAGUAR
The only big cat of the Americas, the jaguar inhabits marshy grassland and wooded riverbanks.

GREAT HORNED OWL
This owl of the Americas hunts in mountains, swamps, and forests. Its head can rotate 180°.

HARPY EAGLE
This massive eagle of the Amazon can swoop at up to 50 mph (80 km/h). It nests in the tallest trees.

MODERATELY DANGEROUS

MODERATELY DANGEROUS

MODERATELY DANGEROUS

Jen and Des Bartlett/Bruce Coleman Ltd.

KINKAJOU

The monkeylike kinkajou has a long prehensile tail that it uses to climb trees and hang on branches.

PORCUPINE

The prehensile tail of the spiny South American porcupine has stiff bristles that help it grip trees.

CAPUCHIN

Central and South America are home to many species of the hairy-headed capuchin monkey.

TWO-TOED SLOTH

Smaller and slightly livelier than the three-toed sloth, it hangs faceup in the trees, hooked on with its claws.

PRAYING MANTIS

This tropical insect uses its hinged forelegs to grab its prey of insects and tiny vertebrates.

TERRITORY

The territorial instincts of animals are usually inspired by two needs: to eat and to breed. An animal may have to defend food resources against others of the same species, and it usually stakes a claim to an area around an actual or proposed breeding site, and defends it against sexual rivals.

FLEXIBLE BOUNDARIES

The food resources of any individual normally extend over a wide area; the animal covers every part of this on a regular basis, and often claims it in some way, such as marking. Despite this, the area is normally too extensive to be defended effectively, and is wholly or partially shared with others. Zoologists call this area the home range.

The breeding area typically lies near the center of the home range; it is much smaller, and the boundaries are sharply defined. The claimant—usually male—defends the area jealously while he is trying to lure a mate; and, once breeding is under way, the area becomes exclusive family property. This is called the territory.

Every mammal has a home range, but it does not necessarily have a territory. Some species are nomadic, ranging widely and never establishing a center of operations. In some cases the territory is

GIANT ANTEATER

*confronting an ocelot.
Normally docile, a
threatened anteater
will rear up and slash
with its claws. Its very
strong forearms can
crush large cats.*

ANTEATERS' HOME RANGE

The size of the home range depends on the richness of the habitat: A giant anteater may find everything it needs within 0.8–1 sq mi (2–3 sq km) of tropical forest, where prey is abundant, but on the semiarid llanos of Venezuela a single giant anteater may range over 9.6 sq mi (25 sq km). The home ranges of tamanduas vary in the same way. Research on Barro Colorado Island, Panama, however, indicates that adult male silky anteaters forage over some 27 acres (11 ha), with no overlap between the ranges of neighboring males. This suggests that the silky anteater has developed a far less relaxed approach to territoriality than the larger species.

Illustration Simon Turvey/Wildlife Art Agency

seasonal: a temporary encampment that is defended for a few months, weeks, or even days. In social animals the situation may be made obvious by frequent, vigorous interactions, but the territorial behavior of solitary species can be hard to pin down.

LONERS AND WANDERERS

All four species of anteaters are essentially solitary animals. They forage and sleep alone, and in the case of tamanduas the two sexes meet only to mate, then go their separate ways. Silky anteaters pair up to raise their young but then part. There is no clan system, no hierarchy, and little social interaction.

> LARGER SPECIES OF ANTEATERS ARE UNPOSSESSIVE ABOUT HOME RANGES AND ARE FAIRLY FRIENDLY WITH EACH OTHER

Anteaters also show a distinctly nomadic tendency. A silky anteater rarely sleeps in the same tree two days in a row, and the giant anteater seems to curl up in any convenient hollow. The tamanduas display no obvious attachment to particular dens. Nursing females carry their young on their backs; in some cases the mother may park her baby in a snug corner while she deals with particularly stubborn prey, but she does not maintain a regular nursery.

So, as far as we know, anteaters—or at any rate the larger species—do not have well-defined territories. They do seem to have home ranges, however, and, if the food supply is less than plentiful, they are capable of depositing scent marks to record their interest in certain areas. ∎

(in)SIGHT

SCENT MARKINGS

Anteaters have developed an acute sense of smell to detect their insect prey, and they may use this in communication. Giant anteaters show interest in the smell of their own saliva, which is often liberally spread around feeding sites, and it is probable that neighbors keep track of each other by monitoring these lingering scents.

Anteaters also have scent-producing anal glands, and in tamanduas the pungency of their anal secretions has earned them a Spanish nickname that translates as "stinkers of the forest." Tamanduas will use this as a weapon and occasionally as a marker.

FOOD AND FEEDING

Ants are among the most numerous of all insects, and any animal that has developed the ability to feed on them will never go hungry. The process of anteating, however, is not easy.

Both ants and termites—which are also eaten by tamanduas—live in colonies defended by stout fortifications, heavily armed soldiers, or both. Their bodies also contain toxic chemicals, some of which have been specially developed as venoms. The quantity of poison in each insect may be small, but since an anteater devours thousands of ants, the cumulative dose is substantial. It has been estimated that an adult male silky anteater feeding on solenopsis ants ingests more than 450 times the amount of venom it would take to kill a dog.

BIZARRE ADAPTATIONS

Acquiring the means to deal with these problems has led to some bizarre adaptations: massive front claws for tearing into ants' nests and termite mounds, immensely long adhesive tongues and beaklike toothless jaws for delving into the nest galleries, and cast-iron digestive systems capable of neutralizing insect toxins. Yet, despite this specialized equipment, anteaters still have problems.

When a giant anteater locates an ants' nest—using its highly developed sense of smell—it tears a hole in it with one of its enlarged front claws, pushes its tubular snout into the breach, and probes deep into the tunnel systems with its wormlike, 24-in (60-cm) tongue. Trapped by the tongue's coating of viscous saliva, the ants are

in SIGHT

ANT ATTACK

The soldier castes of many ants and termites will attack anything that threatens the colony and fight to the death. Most are armed with formidable jaws, and some are capable of injecting painful venoms. Anteaters have no immunity to these weapons. They have been seen interrupting their meals to scratch the swarming, biting insects out of their fur, and they avoid all species with large jaws.

SILKY ANTEATERS *rarely eat termites, but specialize in ants that live in tree branches. They cling to the tree by their tails.*

A GIANT ANTEATER *breaks away the side of a termite mound with its long claws. It uses its 24 in (60 cm) tongue to reach them.*

drawn into the anteater's mouth, crushed against the mouth's horny lining, then swallowed. The process may be repeated some 150 times a minute, enabling the animal to scoop up vast numbers of ants—up to 30,000 ants a day.

The tamanduas feed in much the same way, except that they also forage in the trees for nests of tree-dwelling ants and termites. The silky anteater always feeds in the trees, specializing in

---

ANTEATERS RARELY DESTROY THEIR FOOD RESOURCES, RETURNING TO THE SAME NESTS AGAIN AND AGAIN

---

ants that live among liana stems in the treetops. They eat less than their giant relative, but even a silky anteater can eat up to 5,000 ants a day.

Anteaters rarely prey on scattered foraging ants, since the reward would not justify the effort involved. They always seek out the well-populated nests of favored species. Yet although such a nest may contain all the insects an anteater needs, it never takes more than a small proportion of them before ambling away to find another colony. A giant anteater may visit up to 36 colonies an hour, for eight hours, feeding for about a minute at each.

The reasons for this are not clear. The disturbed ants may retreat into their tunnels, out of range of the anteater's tongue, or the heavily armed soldier ants may rush to the defense of the colony. Whatever the reasons, however, anteaters invariably move on before they can inflict serious damage on a colony. The ants rebuild their defenses, replace their casualties, and carry on. ∎

KEY FACTS

● The tamanduas are the most destructive among the anteaters: They are able to destroy the nests of tree ants by standing on them.

● The giant anteater will sometimes lick water from moist leaves, but it rarely needs to drink. It gets most of the water it needs from the ants it feeds on.

● Since an anteater has no teeth, it cannot chew its food. The insects are pulped in its muscular stomach, which contains grinding stones swallowed for the purpose.

● Tamanduas often switch to a diet of termites at the end of the dry season, just before the breeding termites fly the nest to start colonies of their own. Bigger and fatter than usual, these termites are particularly rich in nutrients.

All illustrations Phillip Hood/Wildlife Art Agency

REPRODUCTION

Giant anteaters and tamanduas both mate in the southern autumn (March to May), timing the event so they give birth in the spring, when they can rely on many months of abundant food. The actual courtship and mating has never been scientifically described and remains something of a mystery. This is partly a reflection of inadequate research, but it also reflects the anteaters' distinctly casual attitude toward the whole business.

PASSING SHIPS

As solitary, seminomadic creatures, anteaters do not enjoy a rich social life. In general, both males and females forage and sleep alone, within their own home ranges. There is no evidence to suggest that males fight for access to females, or that either sex indulges in elaborate courtship procedures. Males and females seem merely to run across one another, mate, and then part—although it is probable that males are attracted by the scent of females in breeding condition.

THE FEMALE GIANT ANTEATER *gives birth standing up, using her tail for support.*

PARASITIC NEMATODES

Parasitic nematodes, also known as roundworms, are some of the most abundant animals on the planet with over 15,000 known species.

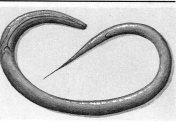

This worm is elongated and tapered at both ends. It is found in every living environment, including plants, and on many animals.

Unusually though, female tamanduas are, in fact, the only mammals known to suffer from infestation with parasitic nematode in their ovaries.

The sexual habits of the silky anteater are even more mysterious, mainly because it lives in the forest canopy, beyond the range of casual observation. But radio tracking indicates that it is more territorial than its larger relatives, with each individual apparently defending its own patch of forest against neighbors of the same sex. The range of each male incorporates that of three females, suggesting a deliberate attempt to monopolize them, but there is no direct evidence of this.

In giant anteaters the gestation is around 190 days, while that of the tamanduas is 130–150

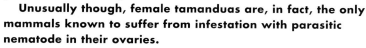

All illustrations Barry Croucher/Wildlife Art Agency

days. The giant anteater gives birth standing upright, propped on her hind legs and tail like a three-legged stool; and the single newborn baby immediately crawls up her fur and onto her back. Fully furred, the young giant anteater is an exact miniature of its mother, and as it rides upon her back its color pattern merges into hers so the two are almost indistinguishable.

By contrast a young tamandua is usually quite different in shade, so it is relatively conspicuous as it clings to its mother's fur.

A young giant anteater relies on its mother's milk for six months, but it may ride on her back for a year or more, feeding alongside her when she cracks into an ants' nest. It is mobile at about the age of four weeks, but if she wanders off it will call her with shrill whistles until she returns. Eventually—up to two years after birth—the young anteater

PRIMITIVE REPRODUCTION

Jany Sauvanet/NHPA

Female anteaters have reproductive and excretory functions both situated in a single chamber. Unlike other mammals, they also have a simple uterus (a single uterine cavity rather than a two-chambered branching organ). The placenta is discoid in shape and is shed at birth. Female anteaters and tamanduas bear only one young at a time and suckle it for six months.

The reproductive life of the silky anteater (*above, with young*) is still largely a mystery.

GIANT ANTEATER (below) *carrying young piggyback style. The mother alone bears the responsibility of raising the offspring.*

achieves independence. By this time it is fully grown and on the verge of sexual maturity, and its mother may be pregnant again.

CARING FOR THEIR YOUNG

The tree-dwelling tamanduas and silky anteaters also carry their young on their backs but often park them in secure corners while they feed. A silky anteater will make a nest in the fork of two branches and place her infant in it while she works on an ant colony. Then she gathers up the baby for the next stage of her night patrol.

Silky anteaters are quite unlike the larger species in that the father helps with raising the young. The parents take turns carrying it, and once it is weaned they both feed it on semidigested insects, regurgitated on demand. As it grows it becomes more adventurous, wandering off while the parents are feeding. For some weeks it feeds within part of its home range, but then it strikes out into the forest to claim a space of its own. ∎

THREATENED BY CHANGE

SUPERBLY ADAPTED FOR THEIR SPECIALIZED LIFESTYLES, ANTEATERS ARE LESS WELL EQUIPPED TO COPE WITH THE EROSION OF THEIR HABITATS BY AN EXPANDING HUMAN POPULATION

C lumsy and slow, bizarre in appearance and quirky in their habits, anteaters may seem ill-qualified for long-term survival. Evolution has molded them for a particular way of life based on the exploitation of a specific type of prey, and history suggests that such specialization makes animals extremely vulnerable to the effects of environmental change.

While their habitats remain intact, such highly adapted species flourish, but the slightest change may irretrievably damage their chances. Many ecosystems are fragile structures based on complex relationships between many organisms; when these relationships are disturbed the whole edifice may tumble down; highly specialized creatures like the anteater are often the first casualties.

> THE GIANT ANTEATER IS THE MOST VULNERABLE OF THE ANTEATERS BECAUSE IT MAKES SUCH AN EASY TARGET FOR HUNTERS

Such disturbance can be caused by natural phenomena such as volcanic eruptions, forest fires, flooding, or, on a longer timescale, climatic change. For many millions of years, however, the anteaters have survived such natural catastrophes and even developed means to exploit them.

VENEZUELAN FLOODS

On the poorly drained llanos of Venezuela, for example, torrential rain leads to widespread flooding during the tropical rainy season, often to a depth of three feet or more. Yet, judging from radio tracking evidence, the foraging patterns of the local giant anteaters do not change at all, and

it is likely that they simply wade through the floodwaters browsing on ants that have been flushed out of their nests by the rising tide. In so doing they switch from one prey species to another, for the species they prefer seem to be less vulnerable to inundation. When the waters recede the anteaters return to their usual diet and habits.

In natural circumstances anteaters are also well able to defend themselves against attack. The massive front claws found on all four species may have evolved as defensive weapons against jaguars, pumas, eagles, and the saber-toothed cats that once prowled the plains and forests of South America. There is plenty of evidence that this is

This Brazilian forest (right) *has been cleared to make way for a soybean crop.*

Partridge Productions/Oxford Scientific Films

Aerial view of farm buildings in the wetlands of the Pantanal, Brazil (above).

Martin Endler/NHPA

This map shows the former and current distribution of the giant anteater.

FORMER DISTRIBUTION   PRESENT DISTRIBUTION

The giant anteater once occurred throughout the lowland grasslands and open forests of Central and South America, from southern Belize and Guatemala to northern Argentina, but today it has been reduced to scattered populations isolated by environmental destruction. The main concentrations are in the national parks of South America where it is protected and, in theory at least, safe from hunting and further habitat erosion.

It is difficult to assess the numbers of the silky anteater. Spending all of its time in the trees, it is difficult to locate—even by the local people.

still their prime function and that they are convenient for ripping into ants' nests. The claws of the giant anteater, in particular, are highly effective against predators, and it is doubtful whether such a large, clumsy, ground-dwelling animal could have survived without them.

Yet although anteaters have developed ways of dealing with dangerous predators and natural events, they seem to be retreating from the threat posed by humans. Once widespread from Guatemala to northern Argentina, the giant anteater—the most visible and easily counted species—is now restricted to scattered, isolated populations and has become extinct in many northern parts of its former range. In remote areas such as the Sierra da Canastra National Park in eastern Brazil, it is still numerous, but wherever the land has been influenced by humans, its numbers have dwindled.

One reason for this is hunting. The giant anteater has no commercial or culinary value, but its weird appearance, size, and sheer visibility make it a tempting target. Those claws may make short work of a puma, but they are no defense against a man with a gun, and since several parts of Central and South America are in a state of civil war, men with guns have become a normal part of everyday life. Random killing is common, and giant anteaters make spectacular trophies.

NO NATURAL ENEMIES

Because it has few natural enemies, the giant anteater is particularly vulnerable to hunting. Animals that are regularly taken as prey by others develop ways of absorbing the losses, usually by breeding rapidly. A female rabbit, for example, can breed at the age of four months, and may produce up to six litters of six young apiece within the year; if she is killed by a predator within five months of birth, she may still leave more than six young behind her.

By contrast a female giant anteater does not become sexually mature until she is two or three years old. When she finally breeds she gives birth

---

THE TAMANDUAS ARE ALSO KNOWN AS LESSER ANTEATERS BECAUSE THEY ARE THE SMALLEST OF THE FAMILY

---

to a single baby, which clings to her back for up to two years and is probably incapable of surviving without her. When it achieves independence, its mother may mate again, giving birth at the age of, say, five, and rearing this second offspring for a further two years. Since each female must raise a minimum of two replacements to maintain population numbers, she must survive for seven years: a long time in a trigger-happy neighborhood.

HABITAT EROSION

Hunting is bad enough, but a more insidious threat is that posed by habitat erosion. Such destruction is not new: Substantial areas of forest in Central America were cleared by the Aztec and Mayan civilizations, and the Spanish conquistadores introduced cattle ranching and cut the tropical hardwoods for export back to the Old World. These activities made little serious impact on the ecosystem, owing to the restricted areas involved, but within the last 50 years the human populations of Central and South America have increased dramatically. The demand for land—for timber, ranching, and agriculture—has increased accordingly, with dramatic consequences.

Nick Gordon/Ardea

ENDANGERED ENVIRONMENT

RAIN FOREST DESTRUCTION

To the north of the great rain forests of Amazonia lie the llanos of northern Colombia and Venezuela: broad, largely treeless grasslands flanking the middle reaches of the Orinoco River and its tributary streams. In the dry season these grassy plains look much like the African savannas, but when the tropical rains come the rivers burst their banks. Because the soils of the llanos are largely composed of thick, impermeable clay, the water cannot drain away, and the landscape becomes flooded.

The giant anteater is one of the dominant mammals of this region. It can cope with the seasonal inundation because it is big enough to wade through the floodwaters—and more importantly because its insect prey can survive by retreating to strong nests or tall vegetation. As long as the grasslands remain intact, the floods of the rainy season are just a

DEFORESTION IS OCCURRING AT AN ALARMING RATE IN CENTRAL AMERICA.

CONSERVATION MEASURES

Public concern regarding the destruction of habitats for cattle ranching is growing rapidly, and more and more people are eating less meat in order to save natural habitats for animals such as anteaters.

Many environmental groups are doing all they can to keep public awareness alive, not only about the loss of habitat through farming, but also about the loss of rain forest for the lucrative hardwood trade. Rain-forest felling carried out on a massive scale in Central and South America has serious temporary inconvenience.

But the llanos is under threat, for large areas have been virtually destroyed by overgrazing. Trampled and bitten down to the quick, the grasses never get a chance to recover and eventually die back. Stripped of its protective vegetation, the soil is blown to dust during the dry season and eroded by floodwater during the rains. The habitat of the grassland ants and termites is swept away, and the livelihood of the giant anteater is swept away with it.

Elsewhere on the plains, cattle ranchers are plowing up the grasslands and reseeding them with imported European grasses, such as rye grass, that are a nutritious source of food for the herds. The plowing, however, is catastrophic for the ant population, and the loss of native plants destroys the natural ecosystem.

Francois Gohier/Ardea

adverse global effects. It causes global warming, which in turn melts the ice caps, causing sea levels to rise and slowly raising temperatures all over the world. This means that the habitats of species everywhere are affected. Fortunately, some governments are now bending to public opinion and are slowly implementing reforestation projects. But the demand for hardwood still flourishes.

ANTEATERS IN DANGER

THE CHART BELOW SHOWS HOW THE INTERNATIONAL UNION FOR THE CONSERVATION OF NATURE (IUCN) CLASSIFIES THE CONSERVATION STATUS OF ANTEATERS. THE YEAR IN PARENTHESES IS THE DATE OF CLASSIFICATION:

GIANT ANTEATER	VULNERABLE (1990)
SOUTHERN TAMANDUA	CITES LISTED (1990)

VULNERABLE MEANS THAT THE SPECIES IS LIKELY TO DECLINE AND BECOME SERIOUSLY ENDANGERED IF NOTHING IS DONE TO IMPROVE ITS SITUATION. *CITES LISTED* MEANS THAT THE SPECIES IS NOT CONSIDERED SUFFICIENTLY AT RISK TO BE ON THE ENDANGERED LIST OF THE IUCN, BUT IT IS LISTED BY THE CONVENTION ON INTERNATIONAL TRADE IN ENDANGERED SPECIES (CITES).

Erwin and Peggy Baeur/Bruce Coleman Ltd.

In Central America over 60 percent of the original forest cover has been swept away, and about 3 percent of the remainder is being destroyed every year by land-hungry peasants. Many of the clearings made for agriculture may eventually revert to secondary forest, but meanwhile the ecosystem is disrupted and the tall forest trees—habitat of the canopy-dwelling silky anteater—will vanish forever.

ELUSIVE SILKY ANTEATER

Being small, elusive, and widespread, the silky anteater is probably in no immediate danger; although if the destruction of the rain forest continues at its present rate, it will succumb along with many of the other forest species. The relatively adaptable tamanduas have often been seen foraging over farmland, and their talent for exploiting temporary opportunities may help them cope with rapid changes as farmers and foresters come and go. Out on the grasslands, however, the giant anteater could soon be in serious trouble.

The main problem is isolation. The wildlife reserves that are now the main refuges of the giant anteater were originally surrounded by vast tracts of natural grassland. The actual boundaries of the reserves were academic, and the anteaters that enjoyed protection within each reserve were able to move in and out, ranging over wide areas and interbreeding at will.

Today much of the grassland outside the reserves has been radically altered and degraded, greatly reducing its value as anteater habitat. Consequently, the anteaters tend to stay within the reserve boundaries, where prey is plentiful. In one respect this is good, since hunting is outlawed

ALONGSIDE MAN

Giant anteaters are relatively popular zoo exhibits. Fed on concoctions of raw meat, beaten egg, milk, and meal, they have survived for over 25 years in captivity. Despite this there have been few breeding successes with the other species.

This probably reflects the impossibility of mimicking an anteater's natural habitat. Duplicating habitats is often difficult, but some species are harder to please than others. Highly specialized creatures require a great deal of study to meet their expectations in captivity.

Andre Bartschi/Planet Earth Pictures

Kenneth W. Fink/Ardea

Inevitably, casualties occur where humans have extended roads across the anteater's habitat (above).

This giant anteater (left), *showing off its long tongue, is part of a captive breeding program.*

in the national parks. Unfortunately the number of giant anteaters within each reserve may be insufficient to guarantee the long-term survival of the species. Isolated populations tend to develop genetic defects, which, if unchecked by out breeding with other populations, can cause an inevitable decline into extinction.

Pollution is also another problem in some areas, such as Colombia and parts of Venezuela.

THE CANOPY OR ROOF OF THE FOREST PROVIDES A SAFE, DENSE COVER THAT IS ALMOST INVISIBLE FROM THE GROUND

Although no figures are available, it is estimated that hazardous waste production reached over a million tons (tonnes) in the 1980s. The area also has high acidity in lakes, rivers, and soil. Although rarely a cause of extinction in itself, this type of pollution does upset the balance of ecosystems and destroys habitats.

Luckily, all four species of anteaters are still fairly widespread and not at imminent risk of extinction, so there is no immediate panic. A few well-chosen measures may yet halt the decline of the giant anteater—the most threatened species— and guarantee the survival of this extraordinary creature into the foreseeable future. ∎

INTO THE FUTURE

The erosion of natural habitat in the unprotected regions of Central and South America is unlikely to slow down in the near future, so the best chance for the continued survival of the four anteater species lies in the maintenance and creation of national parks and wildlife refuges.

Surprisingly, perhaps, some of the small, relatively poor nations of the American tropics have shown more willingness to conserve large areas of wilderness than many of the richer nations of the

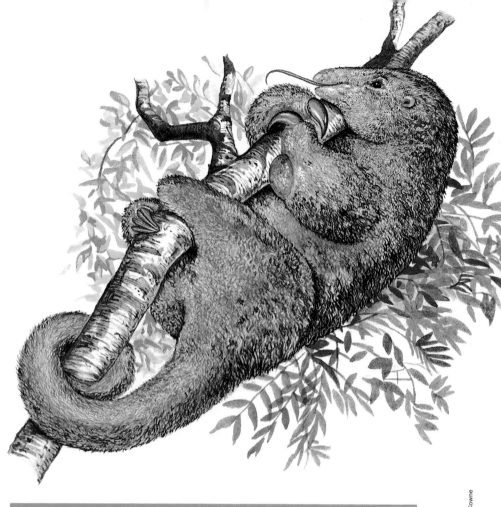

Illustration Joanne Cowne

PREDICTION

THE SILKY ANTEATER'S FATE

The toylike features of the silky anteater have saved it from being killed for sport. But, ironically, its cuteness has put its future in jeopardy from the pet trade worldwide.

developed world. Costa Rica is a shining example, with some 10 percent of the total land area designated for conservation. Since three of the four anteater species occur in Costa Rica—the giant anteater, silky anteater, and northern tamandua—the policy has obviously benefited the anteater family considerably.

But Costa Rica represents only a tiny fraction of the total range of the anteaters, and elsewhere in Latin America the conservation policy has been far less thorough.

Although the area protected by law throughout the region has increased eightfold since 1970, many of the reserves are poorly managed and inadequately policed; local exploitation of the natural resources is frequent and widespread, and the fragile nature of many of the habitats involved means that the damage caused by such exploitation is often irreversible. ■

PREDICTION

ANTEATERS AND DRUG BARONS

In countries such as Colombia, the central government places high priority on policies concerning the illegal cocaine trade; thus, commitment to conservation may be annulled at any time.

HIGH NUMBERS

A study of the giant anteater in Sierra da Canastra National Park in Brazil concluded that the animals were more numerous, and a more important element of the local ecology, than had once been supposed. The population density was calculated from sightings obtained over a limited area 90 to 30 minutes before sunset—the anteaters' most active period.

Sierra da Canastra is a remote area with few large predators, so the anteaters may find the conditions to their liking and flourish accordingly. Nevertheless, the figures could indicate that the current view of this anteater's vulnerability is a little pessimistic.

SAFE HAVENS

Wildlife authorities in Latin America are looking at ways to improve the effectiveness of the national park as a wildlife refuge. One suggestion involves establishing buffer zones around the protected areas. Limited exploitation of the natural resources would be permitted in these zones, but all hunting and severely disruptive activity would be banned. This should enable the animals to flourish outside the park boundaries and would greatly reduce encroachment into the parks themselves. Another idea involves paying cash rewards to farmers and ranchers who agree to set aside a portion of their land for wildlife conservation; but since cash is in short supply in many of the countries involved, this may prove unaffordable.

ANTELOPES

A. & M. Shah/Planet Earth Pictures

TRIBES OF THE SAVANNA

AT FIRST GLANCE MOST SPECIES OF ANTELOPE LOOK REMARKABLY LIKE DEER. BUT THEY ARE, IN FACT, MEMBERS OF THE CATTLE FAMILY

A mong the many species of herbivorous hoofed animals that make up the mammal order Artiodactyla are antelopes. They are part of the cattle family, or Bovidae, distinguished by the fact that the males have horns that are never shed. If a horn is broken, it never regrows properly.

The fossil history of the bovids goes back 25 million years to the early Miocene in Africa. By the middle of this epoch, bovids had invaded Asia and

by the Pleistocene epoch, two million years ago, they had found their way into North America.

WHISTLERS AND JUMPERS

Grazing antelopes form the subfamily Hippotraginae. In this family, reedbuck, rhebok, and waterbuck make up the tribe Reduncini, of which all nine species are confined to Africa. The three species of reedbuck are light and graceful animals, characterized by whistling and high bouncing

Grazing antelope and spiral-horned antelope are members of the cattle family, Bovidae, which comprises over 130 species, of which 75 are found in Africa. The family is divided into several subfamilies and tribes.

ORDER

Artiodactyla
(hoofed mammals)

FAMILY

Bovidae
(cattle)

SUBFAMILY

Hippotraginae
(grazing antelope)

TRIBES

Reduncini
(nine species)
Alcelaphini
(eight species)
Hippotragini
(seven species)

SUBFAMILY

Bovinae
(wild cattle and
spiral-horned
antelope)

TRIBE

Strepsicerotini
(nine species)

Topis prefer grassland habitats, and their long narrow muzzles are adapted for selective feeding.

jumps. Their head and body measurement is 43–63 in (110–160 cm). The body hair color varies from light fawn to grayish and is short and stiff. Like all the members of the tribe, only the males have horns.

The single species of rhebok has a head and body measurement of 45–50 in (115–125 cm), and its brownish gray coat is longer and curlier than the coats of other antelopes.

The remaining members of the tribe are the waterbuck and its close relatives, the kob, puku, and two species of lechwe. These water-loving creatures are medium- to large-sized animals with a relatively heavy gait. The largest is the shaggy waterbuck, which measures 70–93 in (177–235 cm).

CLOSE TO CATTLE

The tribe Alcelaphini, consisting of gnu, harte-beests and impalas, are grazing antelope found in high population densities in parts of southern Africa.

The gnu, more commonly known as wildebeests, are large cattlelike antelope, with a head-and-body length of 60–95 in (150–240 cm) and a shoulder height of 40–58 in (100–145 cm). The coat of the black wildebeest, or white-tailed gnu, is dark brown to black, while that of the blue wildebeest, or brindled gnu, is grayish silver. Both sexes have horns, which grow out sideways and slightly forward, curving sharply upward at the ends. They move around in vast herds.

There are two species of hartebeests, the largest being the Lichtenstein's hartebeest, which may

The eland (above) *is the largest of the antelopes. A fully grown bull can weigh up to 2,000 lb (900 kg).*

Gordon Langsbury/Bruce Coleman Ltd.

Jonathan Scott/Planet Earth Pictures

The kudu (below) *has large ears that are highly sensitive to the sound of enemies approaching.*

Mary Clay/Planet Earth Pictures

measure over 80 in (200 cm). However, with a shoulder height of up to 60 in (150 cm), the other species, known just as the hartebeest, is often taller. The coloration of this species ranges from brownish gray to chestnut while Lichtenstein's hartebeest is a yellowish tawny color.

There is only one species of impala. The head and body of this graceful animal measure 44–50 in (110–150 cm), and it stands 31–40 in (78–100 cm) high at the shoulder. Its coat is glossy, with dark fawn to reddish upper parts and a distinctive black streak running down each side of the rump. The horns are lyre shaped. Other members of the tribe Alcelaphini include the bontebok, blesbok, topi, or tsessebe, and hirola or Hunter's hartebeest.

HORSELIKE ANTELOPES

The dry regions of Africa are the province of the Hippotragini, a tribe of horselike antelope that includes the Arabian oryx, scimitar oryx, gemsbok (also a species of oryx), addax, roan antelope, and sable antelope. The largest of this group are the roan and sable antelope, which have a head-and-body measurement of up to 105 in (267 cm) and can stand up to 64 in (160 cm) at the shoulder. Roan antelopes are pale reddish brown, while sable antelopes vary from rich chestnut to black. Both sexes have horns, which are stout and straight.

The three species of oryx have a head-and-body measurement of 60–94 in (150–235 cm) and may stand up to 56 in (140 cm) at the shoulder. Adult coloration varies from cream to gray or brown, and there is a distinct mane down the back of the neck. Both sexes have horns, but the horns of the females are longer and more slender.

inSIGHT

ASIAN TRIBE

Peninsular India is home to the antelope tribe Boselaphini, which contains just two species, the four-horned antelope and the nilgai. The four-horned antelope is a small animal, with a head-and-body measurement of only 25 in (100 cm). The front pair of horns is 0.8–1.6 in (2–4 cm), while the hind pair is located further back on the head and is 3.2–4 in (8–10 cm) long. This species is found in wooded, hilly country near water.

Its relative the nilgai is a large antelope (the largest found in Asia) measuring up to 84 in (210 cm) and weighing up to 660 lb (300 kg). It inhabits forests, low jungles, and sometimes open plains. The male has a bluish coat (nilgai means "blue bull or cow").

The species that is best adapted to life in the desert is the addax as it has widely splayed hooves —an adaptation for walking on desert sand.

SPIRAL HORNS

Spiral-horned antelopes make up the tribe Strepsicerotini in the subfamily Bovinae. Seven of the nine species within this tribe belong to the same genus, *Tragelaphus*. They are: the greater and lesser kudu, the nyala and mountain nyala, the sitatunga, bushbuck, and bongo. The other two species are the common eland and the giant eland.

The largest of these animals is the mountain nyala, which has a head-and-body length of up to 104 in (260 cm). Its coat is shaggy and grayish chestnut in color, with poorly defined white stripes on back and upper flanks. Other species have more clearly defined white marks; the bongo and both species of kudu have pale stripes down their sides. The horns of all the members of this group are more or less spiral in shape. ∎

THE ANTELOPES' FAMILY TREE

The African grazing antelope, spiral-horned antelope, Asian four-horned antelope, and nilgai belong to various tribes within the much larger Bovidae or cattle family. In fact, cattle as we know them evolved from animals resembling the present-day four-horned antelope and the nilgai (tribe Boselaphini) found in peninsular India.

IMPALA
Aepyceros melampus
(Aae-pie-SER-os mel-AMP-us)

The impala is often described as "the perfect antelope." It is the dominant antelope found in less fertile woodlands of central and southern Africa. Classified within the same tribe as these graceful animals are the impressive gnu or wildebeest, hartebeest, bontebok, topi, and hirola.

TRIBE
ALCELAPHINI

FOUR-HORNED ANTELOPE
Tetracerus quadricornis
(Te-tra-SER-rus kwod-ree-COR-nees)

The four-horned antelope and the nilgai (Boselaphus tragocamelus) are the only members of this tribe. The four-horned antelope occurs in India, while the nilgai is found in India, Nepal, and eastern Pakistan.

TRIBE
BOSELAPHINI

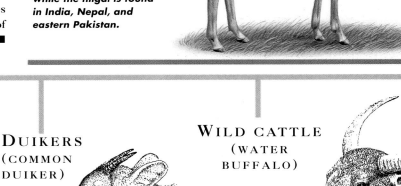

GAZELLES
(DORCAS GAZELLE)

DUIKERS
(COMMON DUIKER)

WILD CATTLE
(WATER BUFFALO)

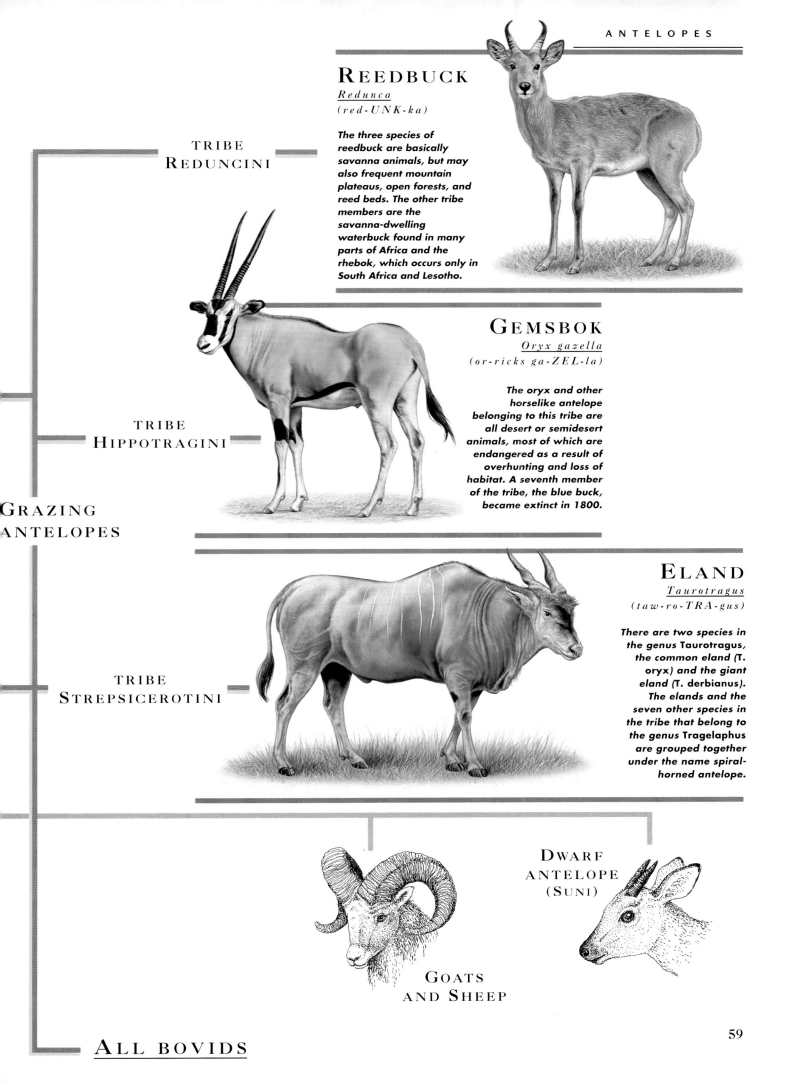

REEDBUCK
Redunca
(red-UNK-ka)

The three species of reedbuck are basically savanna animals, but may also frequent mountain plateaus, open forests, and reed beds. The other tribe members are the savanna-dwelling waterbuck found in many parts of Africa and the rhebok, which occurs only in South Africa and Lesotho.

TRIBE
REDUNCINI

GEMSBOK
Oryx gazella
(or-ricks ga-ZEL-la)

The oryx and other horselike antelope belonging to this tribe are all desert or semidesert animals, most of which are endangered as a result of overhunting and loss of habitat. A seventh member of the tribe, the blue buck, became extinct in 1800.

TRIBE
HIPPOTRAGINI

GRAZING
ANTELOPES

ELAND
Taurotragus
(taw-ro-TRA-gus)

There are two species in the genus Taurotragus, the common eland (T. oryx) and the giant eland (T. derbianus). The elands and the seven other species in the tribe that belong to the genus Tragelaphus are grouped together under the name spiral-horned antelope.

TRIBE
STREPSICEROTINI

DWARF
ANTELOPE
(SUNI)

GOATS
AND SHEEP

ALL BOVIDS

ANATOMY:
THE WILDEBEEST

THE MANE

of the wildebeest is long and tufted and very distinctive. The animal often shakes its mane vigorously during ritual displays.

An adult male blue wildebeest or brindled gnu (above left) is one of the largest antelope (see Fact File). The mountain reedbuck, however, (above right) is the smallest of the reedbuck and has a shoulder height of up to 23 in (76 cm) and a weight of 66 lb (30 kg).

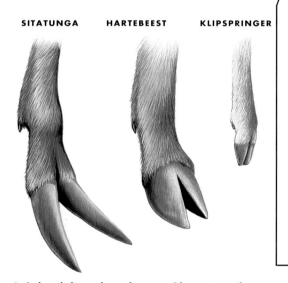

SITATUNGA   HARTEBEEST   KLIPSPRINGER

Artiodactyls have cloven hooves with two toes. The mountain-dwelling klipspringer, a dwarf antelope, has small, pointed hooves for balance. The larger hartebeest and sitatunga have splayed hooves to support their weight on soft ground.

THE HEAD

is massive with a broad muzzle. There are scent glands on the face that are rubbed on the rumps of other wildebeest during social interaction.

THE EARS

are large. Hearing is acute as this animal is the favorite prey of many predators. During courtship the ears are turned downward.

THE HOOVES

are even and slightly splayed in proportion to the weight of this large animal. Wildebeests are always on the move.

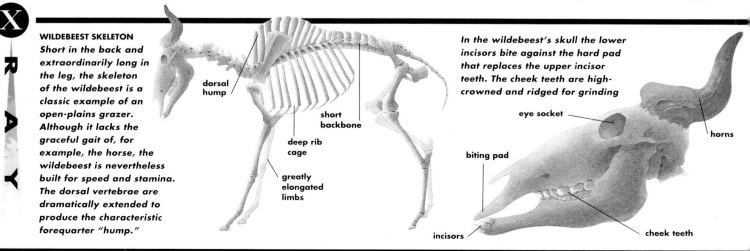

WILDEBEEST SKELETON
Short in the back and extraordinarily long in the leg, the skeleton of the wildebeest is a classic example of an open-plains grazer. Although it lacks the graceful gait of, for example, the horse, the wildebeest is nevertheless built for speed and stamina. The dorsal vertebrae are dramatically extended to produce the characteristic forequarter "hump."

dorsal hump

short backbone

deep rib cage

greatly elongated limbs

In the wildebeest's skull the lower incisors bite against the hard pad that replaces the upper incisor teeth. The cheek teeth are high-crowned and ridged for grinding

eye socket

horns

biting pad

incisors

cheek teeth

X-ray illustrations Elisabeth Smith. B/W Ruth Grewcock

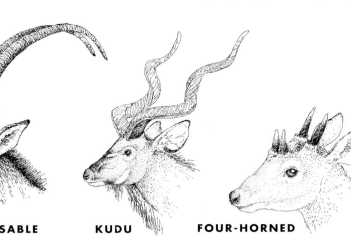

SABLE   **KUDU**   **FOUR-HORNED**

Antelope have evolved different types of horn for varying reasons. The long, curved-back horns of the sable are a means of self-defense, while the spiral horns of the kudu are used in social interaction. The four-horned antelope, the most primitive antelope, has two pairs of horns, one at the front and one at the rear of its head.

FACT FILE:

BLUE WILDEBEEST

CLASSIFICATION

GENUS: *CONNOCHAETES*
SPECIES: *TAURINUS*

SIZE

HEAD–BODY LENGTH: 60–96 IN (150–240 CM)
TAIL LENGTH: 14–22 IN (35–56 CM)
WEIGHT/MALE: 397–606 LB (180–275 KG)
WEIGHT/FEMALE: 309–353 LB (140–160 KG)

COLORATION

GRAYISH SILVER, WITH BROWNISH BANDS ON THE FOREQUARTERS AND NECK
THE FACE AND SCRAGGY MANE ARE BLACK, EXCEPT IN TWO SUBSPECIES, WHICH HAVE VERY OBVIOUS WHITE BEARDS
CONSPICUOUS BLACK TAIL

FEATURES

OXLIKE AND MISLEADINGLY FEROCIOUS IN APPEARANCE
BOTH SEXES HAVE HORNS, WHICH ARE HEAVY AND CURVED
THE HEAD IS MASSIVE WITH A BROAD MUZZLE
THE FEMALES HAVE FOUR MAMMAE
FORELEGS MUCH HEAVIER THAN HIND LEGS

THE BODY

appears clumsy and "front heavy," giving it the appearance of a buffalo. Wildebeests rub their heads on each other's rumps as a form of scent marking.

THE TAIL

is black and highly visible. The wildebeest is often described as the clown of the plains, as it cavorts about, lashing its tail vigorously. This may help to attract the attention of females, and certainly is an efficient flyswatter.

THE LEGS

are long and elegant. As in most antelopes, this streamlining means that wildebeest are fast runners.

humerus

BUSHBUCK SKULL
This typical spiral-horned antelope has a long, narrow face. The lower incisors project forward, and the cheek teeth have ridges of enamel on the crown.

horns

narrow skull

projecting incisors

high-crowned cheek teeth

ANTELOPE FORELIMBS
An antelope's legs have evolved to provide speed and endurance. Have a look at your hand and feel the bones between the wrist and knuckles; these are the metatarsals. On an antelope, the outer two metatarsals have been lost, while the central two have fused to become the single, long "cannon bone." The splayed hooves sit at the tips of the "fingers."

elbow joint

ulna (forearm)

wrist

"cannon bone" (central two metatarsals)

cloven hoof with two "fingers"

Main illustration Kim Thompson

SAFETY IN NUMBERS

GRAZING ANTELOPE ARE AT THEIR MOST VULNERABLE WHEN FEEDING ON THE OPEN PLAINS. THEY TEND TO STAY IN GROUPS AND HAVE DEVELOPED A SPECTACULAR SIGNALING SYSTEM TO WARN OF DANGER

A nimals that live out in the open are easily seen and are therefore extremely vulnerable to predators. To counter this they tend to move around in herds, which in the case of some species can be huge. Unlike most other bovids, members of the related subfamily Bovinae, or wild cattle, are nonterritorial.

GETTING AROUND

In order to get from one place to another, the alcelaphines, which include gnu or wildebeests, hartebeests, and impalas, either amble or canter. Trotting is reserved for play or as an alarm signal. The signal is emphasized by lifting the legs high and lashing the tail. When alarmed, the bontebok, blesbok, topi, and hirola tend to bounce straight up

MOST BOVIDS ARE GREGARIOUS ANIMALS THAT RELY ON THE FACT THAT THERE IS SAFETY IN NUMBERS

into the air with all four legs held straight down. A herd of hartebeests often has a sentinel posted in order to warn the others of danger. When alarmed, the animals gallop away in a single file.

The most spectacular reaction to danger is that of a herd of impalas, which can make prodigious leaps. In one case, an impala was seen to make successive leaps of 26, 16, and 30 ft (8, 5, and 9 m). Impala spend much of their time among bushes, and they can escape with ease by leaping over obstacles. However, they also leap high into the air when there are no obstacles to overcome; this is often to display their strength to an enemy. Reedbuck are also noted for their ability to leap, even through shallow water. They also bounce up and down when extremely agitated.

Antelope are generally diurnal. Most members

of the horselike Hippotragini tribe, for example, may be seen moving about and feeding at any time of the day or night, although periods of peak activity are necessarily at the coolest times of the day and in the middle of the night.

The spiral-horned bushbuck and kudu may also be active both during the day and at night. Their reputation for being nocturnal in places is probably due to the fact that human predation has caused them to become wary and secretive.

Wildebeests and other alcelaphines that graze in open country tend to do most of their grazing during daylight hours rather than at night, when the risk of being caught unawares by a predator is much greater. Among the reduncines, the waterbuck, kob, lechwe, and puku stay hidden in cover

R. de la Harpe/Planet Earth Pictures

Steve Robinson/NHPA

Impalas (above) *can make leaps of up to 30 ft (9 m) when in flight—often for no apparent reason.*

- No animal can run faster through water than a lechwe. Its gait, in which fore and hind feet move in pairs, looks clumsy on land, but is highly efficient in mud and shallow water.

- Eland appear to fear only humans. They attack all other potential threats, such as baboons, warthogs, and lions.

- If a reedbuck is disturbed, by a leopard, for example, it whistles in alarm and will continue doing so for up to half an hour after the coast is clear.

- The bushbuck is built for rushing, bounding, and dodging through cover. In open ground it lacks stamina.

during the night and come out to graze during the day. Their close relative, the reedbuck, on the other hand, does exactly the opposite.

Communication between individuals is achieved by methods similar to those found in most grazing and browsing animals. Scent is nearly as important as sight for recognizing other individuals, and a stranger will be checked out very thoroughly, using both eyes and nose. In migratory species, such as wildebeests, scent from hoof glands help individuals keep track of one another. Nonterritorial species, of course, do not need to mark the ground using scent, dung, or urine, and even some of the more territorial antelope, such as reedbuck, do not deliberately leave scent marks.

NOISES OFF!

Bushbuck, kudu, and eland greet each other with a gruff bark. This appears to advertise both sex and status and when necessary acts as an alarm call. Reedbuck and kobs whistle, while lechwe grunt. The waterbuck snorts when alarmed, but otherwise remains relatively silent. Hartebeests and their relatives are also fairly quiet, but they do produce calls that sound like grunts or quacks. Female wildebeests low like cattle, but the males produce very different sounds. The black wildebeest produces a hiccup noise, while the common wildebeest gets its alternative name—the gnu—from a metallic grunt that sounds like "hnou." ∎

A young nyala leaves the safety of dense foliage to drink water. It must be ever alert for predators.

HABITATS

Antelope are found in nearly all kinds of tropical and subtropical habitats, from mountain forest through lowland rain forest, wooded and open savanna to arid mountains and desert.

WOODLAND DWELLERS

Of the five tribes of antelope, forest and woodland dwellers are mostly found among the spiral-horned antelope of the tribe Strepsicerotini. These animals are opportunistic in their feeding, giving them an advantage over more specialized feeders. For example, although the giant eland, which occurs in the sub-Saharan zone from Senegal to southern Sudan, is a woodland animal, the common eland, which occurs from Ethiopia to South Africa, is found in wood and grassland.

The mountain nyala inhabits forest and heathland at heights of 9,500–12,500 ft (2,900–3,800 m) in the highlands of southern Ethiopia. Its relative, the nyala, which occurs in southern Malawi, Mozambique, Zimbabwe, and eastern South Africa, is found at lower elevations. It prefers to be near water and needs dense cover for protection. The two species of kudu also inhabit dense bush and woodland. The greater kudu occurs

> THE SMALLER SPIRAL-HORNED ANTELOPES HAVE LITTLE SPEED AND STICK TO DENSE COVER FOR PROTECTION

from southern Chad eastward to Somalia and southward to South Africa. The lesser kudu occurs in northeastern Africa in an area that includes the Arabian peninsula, Ethiopia, southeastern Sudan, Somalia, northeastern Uganda, Kenya, and eastern Tanzania. The sitatunga is semiaquatic. It occurs from Gambia eastward to southern Sudan and southward to northern Botswana, and it lives in dense, swampy reed beds.

VERSATILE GRAZERS

Grazing antelope tend to be found where grass is plentiful. However, this does not make them any less versatile. They have colonized every habitat from the flooded swamps of the Nile Sudd to the almost plantless regions of the Sahara desert and windswept pastures, which on Mt. Kilimanjaro reach up to 16,400 ft (5,000 m).

The most aquatic members of this group are the reduncines, most of which are found near water. The lechwe, for example, is restricted to

The waterbuck (above) is possibly the most water dependent of all antelope. As a result, its habitat is limited and territorial competition between males for females is highly intense.

DISTRIBUTION

Africa's diverse grasslands are home to the grazing antelope. The three tribes contained within the subfamily Hippotraginae have colonized every type of habitat. Most reduncines, however, favor wetlands and tall grasslands, while the alcelaphines are grazers of moist grassland and open woodland. The horselike hippotragines can be found in some of Africa's most arid zones. The addax, for example, occurs in the sandy and stony centers of the Namib and Sahara deserts.

The spiral-horned antelope have a less extensive range than the grazing antelope. The boselaphines—the nilgai and the four-horned antelope—are found only in peninsular India.

Trevor Barrett/Bruce Coleman Ltd.

KEY FACTS

● The sitatunga is a good swimmer and may submerge completely when feeding in water. When danger threatens, it can hide underwater, with only its nostrils exposed.

● The Arabian oryx is said to be able to detect rainfall over a great range. It then travels long distances to take advantage of the vegetation that the rain encourages to grow.

● The addax is the most desert-adapted of all antelope species. It lives most of its life without drinking, being able to extract all the water it needs from the plants it eats.

● The bongo runs swiftly through even the thickest cover. To prevent its long horns from becoming caught in the undergrowth, it raises its head so that they lie along its back. As a result, older animals invariably have bare patches on their backs.

● The feet of a sitatunga are specially adapted for walking on marshy ground. The hooves are greatly elongated, the feet are bare, and the foot joints are unusually flexible.

floodplains and nearby ground. Kob and puku inhabit moist savanna, floodplains, and the edges of woodlands near rivers and lakes. Waterbuck, which occur in all the African savanna zones south of the Sahara, are, despite their name, less dependent on water and range farther into wood-lands than other species. The three species of reedbuck also usually live near water, but seldom enter it. They frequent grasslands, mountain plateaus, and open woods as well as reed beds.

Alcelaphines mostly inhabit drier regions. Wildebeests, for example, inhabit open grassy

Lechwe specialize in abundant and highly nutritious grasses near rivers. So keen are they to reach this food that they will wade into water up to their necks.

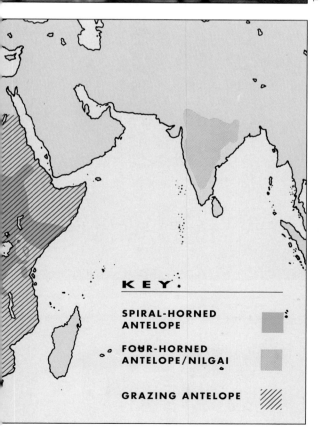

KEY.

SPIRAL-HORNED ANTELOPE

FOUR-HORNED ANTELOPE/NILGAI

GRAZING ANTELOPE

Gert Behrens/Ardea

plains, preferably with a nearby source of water available. The black wildebeest occurs in central and eastern South Africa, while the blue wildebeest is found farther north, from northern South Africa to southern Kenya and southern Angola.

The hartebeest occurs in dry savanna. It was formerly found in much of Africa, but is now restricted to Ethiopia and parts of Botswana, Namibia, Tanzania, and Kenya. Its relative, Lichtenstein's hartebeest, is also a savanna herbivore, but prefers open woodland and floodplain grassland. It occurs in Tanzania, southeastern Zaire, northeastern Angola, eastern Zimbabwe, Malawi, and Mozambique.

The impala favors open country from Kenya and southern Angola to northern South Africa. It avoids the more open areas and is generally found in open woodland or acacia and bush savanna.

Open grassland also includes the bontebok and blesbok of South Africa, the hirola of eastern Kenya and southwestern Somalia, and the topi, which occurs over a large area from Senegal to Ethiopia southward to South Africa.

The driest regions of all are inhabited by members of the Hippotragini tribe. Roan and sable antelope are savanna animals of southern Africa, but gemsbok and oryx inhabit arid, semidesert

Jonathan Scott/Planet Earth Pictures

AFRICA'S SEASONAL GRASSLANDS

Africa's grasslands lie in a huge prairie that stretches from the cold steppes of the southern tip of the continent, northward through the woodlands, wooded and open savannas of equatorial Africa, to the Sahara. This grassland contains an enormous range of wildlife. The Serengeti National Park, for example, is home to over half a million wild animals, most of which are grazing herbivores. These vast herds survive because they seldom compete with one another for food. Also, because of the local climate, they make regular migrations to find fresh food, thus allowing grazed areas to recover.

Herds of grazing antelope spend the wet season (January–June) on the southeastern plains. At the start of the dry season they migrate westward to where the rainfall is greater and the grass longer. In each area there is a grazing succession. First, the zebra arrive to graze the tops of the grass. Then the antelope graze and trample the remaining grass, allowing smaller animals, such as gazelles, to feed on seeds and young shoots at ground level.

DROUGHTS IN AFRICA

Droughts have caused much hardship and death in sub-Saharan Africa. In 1984 and 1985, severe drought struck 150 million people and caused one million deaths. The problem has been compounded by overfarming and deforestation. Also, sparse rain at the best of times has put the people of Africa at the mercy of the elements.

NUMBER OF YEARS OF DROUGHT FACED BY EACH COUNTRY IN THE 1980s

▨ 2 YEARS

▨ 3–5 YEARS

regions. The gemsbok occurs from Ethiopia and Somalia to Namibia and eastern South Africa. The scimitar oryx use to occur in the semidesert parts of Morocco and Senegal westward to Egypt and Sudan. The Arabian oryx formerly inhabited the Middle East and the Arabian peninsula.

The addax used to be found in desert and semidesert areas from the western Sahara and Mauritania to Egypt and Sudan. It travels great distances to find enough of the meager supply of desert plants. Despite the harshness of its habitat it is said to always appear in good condition. ∎

NEIGHBORS

The grasslands of Africa are vast and can support many species. The diversity of vegetation and the adaptability of many animals mean that there is usually enough food to go around.

PLAINS ZEBRA

Zebras can eat the coarsest grasses that are passed over by other animals.

SECRETARY BIRD

The secretary bird eats snakes, and its tough skin prevents bites.

Illustrations Elisabeth Smith, Wayne Ford, and Craig Robson/Wildlife Art Agency

DRY BUSH/THICKET

MOIST (EQUATORIAL)

FOREST/WOODLAND

This simplified map shows how the term "savanna" can describe many different types of African grassland, depending on which particular vegetation dominates each climatic or geographical zone.

ENEMIES

LION
This primary predator of the African savanna is one of the wildebeests' greatest enemies.

CROCODILE
Many water-loving antelope, such as the lechwe, fall prey to crocodiles when they wade in water in search of aquatic vegetation.

TERMITES

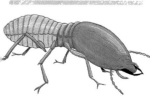

A termite mound is both an impregnable fortress and a protective "microclimate."

WEAVER BIRD

Weaver birds, as their name suggests, build complex, ingenious nests.

JACKAL

This scavenger resembles the domestic dog and may have been its ancestor.

SPITTING COBRA

When cornered, cobras eject venom from fangs up to a distance of 7 ft (2 m).

KORI BUSTARD

This is the heaviest of all flying birds weighing up to 50 lb (22.6 kg).

FOOD AND FEEDING

Being members of the cattle family, antelope are ruminants; that is, they have four stomach chambers and they chew the cud. The part of the stomach known as the rumen contains bacteria that help break down the tough, cellulose cell walls of plants. The contents of the rumen are regularly brought back up into the mouth for further chewing. This process, known as chewing the cud, helps break down the food even further.

BROWSERS AND GRAZERS

Antelope are either browsers or grazers. Among African antelope there are often clear anatomical differences between the two; in Africa, grasses are very tough, while tree and shrub leaves often produce defensive poisonous chemicals.

Most of the African antelopes, therefore, specialize in particular types of food, and they tend to go hungry when their preferred food becomes scarce. There are, however, a few species that are able to exploit almost any source of food.

Members of the Strepsicerotine tribe, that is, spiral-horned antelope, are inhabitants of the most productive habitats—tropical rain forests and woodlands—and, therefore, tend to be opportunistic feeders that exist on a varied diet. The bongo, for example, browses on the shoots and growing tips of many plants. It is especially fond of the leaves of bamboo, cassava, and sweet

---

SPIRAL-HORNED ANTELOPE ARE FOLIAGE GLEANERS IN THAT THEY ALWAYS FIND RICH PICKINGS IN POOR VEGETATION

---

potato plants and has been known to raid plantations of coco yams in order to eat the leaves. Like many other browsing animals it can reach high into trees by rearing up on its hind legs and bracing its front legs against a tree trunk. It is said to eat earth and chew pieces of burned wood from trees that have been struck by lightning, apparently to obtain salt.

Most other members of the tribe have similar diets of leaves and shoots, although the bushbuck grazes grass and eland eat fruit. The semiaquatic sitatunga grazes reeds, sedges, and grasses.

Most of the reduncines are grazers; only the rhebok browses. In the moist habitats frequented by reedbuck, waterbuck, kob, puku, and lechwe, grass is generally plentiful, although some species may make local migrations. For example, the

Color Illustrations Evi Antoniou

kob, which feeds on short grasses in lightly wooded grasslands during the wet season, may move 90–120 miles (150–200 km) to find patches of grass along watercourses during dry seasons.

SPECIALIZED GRAZERS

Lechwe, the most specialized of the reduncines, generally graze while standing in 2–8 in (5–20 cm) of water, although some venture so far in the water that their backs are covered. Reedbuck seldom stray far from water, and in farming areas they often invade young cereal crops. Waterbuck graze on short and medium-length grasses and reeds. They normally keep to the shallows, but during the dry season they will wade in deeper to browse on aquatic vegetation. A varied diet means that individuals can stay in a small area.

Some of the grazing alcelaphines of the African savanna, though, make long migrations. As the food runs out in one place they move to another, allowing the grass to regrow in the area they have left behind. Wildebeests, which feed on succulent plants and karro bushes as well as grass, are noted for their migratory habits,

Ferrero Labat/Ardea

THE BUSHBUCK

(below) *is normally found in dense woodland, but it is an opportunistic feeder and will also use local cover in otherwise open grassland to exploit a wide range of habitats.*

THE FOUR-HORNED ANTELOPE

(right) *inhabits wooded, hilly areas rich in foliage. They need to drink frequently and so are always to be found near rivers and streams.*

Impala are opportunist feeders. They travel in large groups and will even eat flowers and fruit.

although some small herds may stay in one place all year, moving as little as 0.3 sq miles (1 sq km).

Topi specialize in the green grass of valley bottoms but will also feed on other plants, as do the bontebok and hirola. Hartebeests are less selective, but are exclusively grazers, while impalas are both grazers and browsers. During the wet season an impala's diet consists of over 90 percent grass, but changes to around 70 percent herbs and leaves in the dry season. As a result, a herd of impalas can find sufficient food all year round.

FLEXIBLE FEEDERS

Most hippotragines, because of their arid habitats, must be highly flexible when it comes to feeding. Sable antelope are grazers, but browse during the dry season. The addax seems to survive well on the scant Saharan vegetation and never needs to drink. Oryx and gemsbok also feed on sparse grass and the shoots of stunted shrubs. They prefer to have water but can also survive without it for a long time by feeding on melons and bulbs, which they unearth with their front feet. Arabian oryx have been seen eating fruits of the colocynth, or bitter apple, which are poisonous to humans. ■

THE ELAND
(bottom) *digests leaves by chewing the cud. This means that food is regurgitated and chewed over to break it up.*

THE NYALA
(below) *only browses riverside thickets, so it tends to starve when the food source runs out.*

SOCIAL STRUCTURE

Animals in large groups interact more with one another than those that live alone or in small groups. This has led to the development of ritualized behavior and a hierarchical social structure.

Strepsicerotines live alone or in small groups. For example, some 60 percent of sitatunga live alone, the rest living in small, all-female groups.

Eland normally live in groups of about twenty-five. Although social structure is loose, dominance hierarchies exist, and when two individuals meet, relative rank is established, although fighting is rare.

MEET AND GREET

Reduncines are generally much more gregarious; waterbuck, lechwe, kob, and puku are found in herds of thousands. The intricate social structure varies in species. Young male waterbuck, for example, leave their mothers at the age of eight to nine months to form bachelor groups of two to five individuals. Within these groups dominance hierarchy is based on size, strength,

and horn length, and fighting is common.

Kob and lechwe are found in more seasonal habitats and so are less likely to establish permanent territories. Instead, the males gather in a cluster of very small territories known as a lek.

Members of the alcelaphine tribe may also form large groups. During the dry season thousands of wildebeests, of all ages and both sexes, may congregate in the same area. Males compete with one another using ritualized displays and

TOPI BACHELOR
males huddling as a prelude to a sparring contest (below). *In the mating season, topi are found constantly trying to herd together "wards" of females and drive away other males.*

A BOHOR REEDBUCK
advertises its presence (left). *Males tend to be solitary, and the social structure of the species is rather weak.*

HARTEBEEST
bulls tangle horns to defend territory and to assert social hierarchy (right). *The winner will be the stronger bull with the bigger horns. Bulls tend to defend small ranges.*

Color illustrations Robin Budden/Wildlife Art Agency

loud "hnou" calls. They may push one another with their horns, but they seldom fight.

Hartebeests have four social classes: territorial adult males, nonterritorial adult males, bachelor groups, and females and young. When vying for territory males leap forward on their knees.

Impalas are territorial only during wet seasons. The sexes form groups of females and their young, and bachelor males. Each herd of females and young contains 10–100 individuals, with a home range of 0.77–2.32 sq miles (2–6 sq km). However, several herds appear to be associated with a still larger group, or clan. The home ranges of members of a clan may overlap by as much as 73 percent, but the home ranges of different clans do not overlap by more than four percent. ■

BULL TOURNAMENTS

Living in arid environments has caused the Arabian oryx to develop a very tight social structure. There are usually less than 20 individuals in a herd, which is closed to outsiders, and members use their horns to drive off all competitors for the scant desert resources. The group has a strict hierarchy in which bulls usually rank over cows, although some bulls may be dominated by high-ranking cows. This has led to a highly ritualized "tournament" in which members of the herd run around in circles, occasionally stopping to pace the ground. Although the tournament may involve brief bouts of horn-clashing, oryx do not actually fight. In fact, the dominant bull will actually stop other males leaving the group.

WILDEBEEST

displaying the male low horn threat (right). *This display looks serious but, in fact, these animals seldom fight.*

ARABIAN ORYX

(below) *are always found in long-standing groups of 10–20 animals. Their harsh desert environment means that a group has more chance of survival than a single animal.*

LIFE CYCLE

Nursing mothers and young calves need plenty of food and so calving among antelope is timed to coincide with the most productive seasons. In grasslands, this is the wet season, when the rains bring on a fresh growth of grass. However, in rain forests and tropical wetlands, plant growth is continuous and timing is less important.

The swamp-dwelling sitatunga, for example, breeds throughout the year, although each female produces only one offspring about every 12 months. Similarly, the nyala can breed at any time of year, but births tend to peak during the spring and autumn. Little is known about the shy bongo. Births are said to occur in December and January in the wild, although in captivity bongos have given birth in April and August.

MATING AND BIRTH

The eland, though, has distinct breeding seasons in some areas. In Zambia, for example, calves are born in July and August. Like other spiral-horned antelope, eland produce one offspring at a time. It weighs 49–79 lb (22–36 kg) at birth and continues to suckle for four or five months. Males become sexually mature at four years, females at three years. Captive eland have lived for over 23 years.

Among most of the reduncines, breeding may also occur at any time, but the birthrate often peaks at certain times. For example, in Uganda most waterbuck give birth during the two wet seasons, in August and in November and December. The kob population of the Boma region of Sudan produces young mostly at the end of the rainy season in November and December and the

inSIGHT

TONGUE FLASHERS

Male impala have developed an unusual form of foreplay prior to mating. As a dominant male approaches females or rival males, he opens his mouth wide and flicks out his tongue rapidly several times. The response of females to this tongue flashing is to bunch together. On the other hand, males see it as a challenge, to which they react either by fleeing, or by replying with the same display, thus indicating their willingness to accept the challenge to combat.

Color illustrations Nick Pike/Wildlife Art Agency

MALE *impalas form herds for courtship and breeding purposes and gather together 15–25 females for mating* (above). *They spend the rest of their time defending their territory.*

Johnathan Scott/Planet Earth Pictures

YOUNG IMPALAS *are placed in a crèche with adults in attendance and on constant alert for predators* (above). *The lambs are weaned at five to seven months and become sexually mature at 13 months.*

A wildebeest and new calf (left). *The single calf will be born in February–May. This is a vulnerable time for both, so the calf will be up and standing within minutes.*

GROWING UP

The life of a young impala

MATING

occurs at any time of year. It is immediately preceded by an elaborate ritual performed by the male, who will need all his fat reserves for the breeding effort.

GIVING BIRTH

A single young is born six to seven months after the rutting period. Newborn impalas are highly likely to be taken by predators at this time. In fact, the mortality rate is over 50 percent.

stand within 15 minutes of being born and is weaned by the time it is nine months old. Females become sexually mature between one and three years, depending on the size of the herd. Females belonging to large herds tend to mature earlier.

Impalas breed throughout the year, although there are generally two peaks of mating and birth, particularly in South Africa; in equatorial regions, breeding is more continuous. A female impala (ewe) produces a single young (lamb) after a gestation period of six to seven months. The lambs are weaned at five to seven months and males breed at 13 months. Impalas are known to live to over 13 years old in the wild, and a captive impala has reached the age of 17 years.

Addax also breed at any time but mostly in winter or early spring. Oryx and gemsbok do not have special breeding seasons. Gemsbok come into season immediately after giving birth and produce offspring about every nine months. The Arabian oryx produces one calf about once a year under favorable conditions. Gestation takes about eight months, the young are weaned at about 42 months, and the potential life span of oryx and gemsbok seems to be about 20 years. ∎

reedbuck of the Kruger National Park in South Africa mostly between December and May.

The reedbuck of this region live in groups consisting of a mated pair and their young. Male and female separate for three or four months when the female gives birth. She keeps the calf hidden for two months, visiting it for just 10–30 minutes each day to feed it. The bond between mother and calf is broken just before the birth of the next calf, which takes place some nine to 14 months later after gestation of about eight weeks. Females reach sexual maturity between nine and 24 months. One captive reedbuck lived for 18 years.

Mating and birth among wildebeests and hartebeests is highly seasonal—wildebeest calves are born within two or three weeks of the onset of the rainy season. In South Africa this occurs between November and January, while in the Serengeti it takes place in January or February. Females usually produce a single calf after a gestation period of eight to nine months. The calf can

FROM BIRTH TO DEATH

IMPALA
GESTATION: 6–7 MONTHS
LITTER SIZE: 1
BREEDING: ANY TIME, WITH PEAKS IN SPRING AND AUTUMN
WEIGHT AT BIRTH: 8.6–12.1 LB (3.9–5.5 KG)
WEANING: 5–7 MONTHS
LONGEVITY: 13 YEARS

BLUE WILDEBEEST
GESTATION: 8–9 MONTHS
LITTER SIZE: 1
BREEDING: FEBRUARY–APRIL IN SOUTH AFRICA; APRIL–MAY IN THE SERENGETI
FIRST WALKING: 6 MINUTES
WEANING: 9 MONTHS
LONGEVITY: 18–20 YEARS

NO SPACE TO SURVIVE

THE HUNTING OF ANTELOPE FOR MEAT, HIDES, AND SPORT, TOGETHER WITH LOSS OF HABITAT HAS GREATLY REDUCED THE POPULATIONS OF NEARLY EVERY SPECIES, AND MANY ARE NOW ENDANGERED

ike all large herbivores, antelope need a considerable amount of space in which to survive, and the rate at which they reproduce, while adequate under normal circumstances, is not high enough to offset an unusually high mortality rate. As a result, the story of how most of them are surviving in the modern world is all-too-familiar.

THE LUCKY FEW

Probably the least endangered grazing antelope is the blue wildebeest, or brindled gnu. During the 1970s there were an estimated 500,000 of these animals roaming the 9,800 sq miles (25,500 sq km) of the Serengeti and, in contrast to all the other large wild mammals of Africa, the tally has since risen. Today, it is estimated that there are 1–1.5 million blue wildebeests in the Serengeti.

However, this number, together with the 100,000 blue wildebeests in Tanzania, represents over 80 percent of the entire population in Africa. Elsewhere this species has not fared so well. In Botswana, numbers have fallen from hundreds of thousands to around 38,500, because fences erected by farmers have cut off access to water.

The black wildebeest, or white-tailed gnu, of South Africa has been much less successful. During the 19th century this species was almost wiped out by hunters, but, fortunately, small populations were maintained on a few reserves. As a result, it has since been possible to reintroduce the black wildebeest into the wild, and the current population numbers around 10,000.

COMPETING WITH CATTLE

Wildebeests and the other alcelaphines require broadly the same type of grazing and habitat as domestic cattle, with the result that farmers view them as competitors, particularly during the dry season when grazing is more difficult to find. In game parks and reserves this is not a problem, as few domestic cattle are present. Impala populations, for example, are satisfactory and in spite of a certain amount of poaching by hunters, this species is not a cause for concern, particularly as it has been introduced into areas that were once outside its range. Outside such reserves, however, the impala has suffered from overhunting and has disappeared from many parts of southern Africa.

Other alcelaphines have also suffered from loss of habitat as a result of competition with domestic stock. The hirola, for example, is confined to a small area of dry grassland on the border between Kenya and Somalia. During the 1970s the number of cattle that shared its range doubled,

Nigel Dennis/NHPA

Wildebeests at a dry water hole (above). *Many animals die during Africa's harsh droughts.*

Mary Clay/Planet Earth Pictures

This map shows the former and present range of the addax, a horselike antelope of Africa's most arid zones.

FORMER   PRESENT

The addax originally occurred in much of the desert and semidesert region from Mauritania and the western Sahara region across to Sudan and Egypt. Today, however, the only viable herd known to exist is in northeastern Niger. It may contain as many as 200 individuals, or there may now be as few as 50. If the species does become extinct in the wild, there are over 400 individuals in captivity. In theory, therefore, it might be possible to reintroduce it into the wild, but there is no certainty as to how successful such a project might be.

with the result that the Kenyan population decreased by over 75 percent. Estimates in the 1970s suggested that the population was around 14,000, but since then the problems of competition for food and water have been exacerbated by poaching and drought. Today numbers have dropped to between 5,000 and 10,000, and the hirola is officially classified as rare.

The bontebok, which is restricted to a small coastal area of southwestern South Africa, began to decline almost as soon as farmers moved into the region during the early 1800s, as they hunted this species indiscriminately and excluded it from much of its range by enclosing the land on which

The future of the addax hangs in the balance. It is threatened both by hunting and loss of habitat.

they settled. By 1830, the bontebok had all but been exterminated and the species was only saved from extinction by the action of a few farmers who deliberately drove most of the few remaining animals onto their enclosed land in order to preserve them. However, it was not until 1931—100 years later—that the first Bontebok National Park was established, and then with only 17 animals. This, together with the creation of a second park in 1961, allowed the population of bontebok to increase to over 800 by 1970, and today this species numbers around 1,500.

The hartebeest, too, has been greatly reduced in numbers over the years, due, again, to hunting and modification of its habitat. In South Africa it has largely disappeared, and one of the North African subspecies became extinct in the early 1900s. Because it competes directly with cattle for grazing and is particularly easy to hunt, the remaining subspecies have probably suffered a greater contraction of range than any other African ruminant and they are classified as endangered. One of these subspecies, the Tora hartebeest, may also be on the point of extinction as a result of the severe drought that caused such devastation in Ethiopia and Sudan in the early 1980s. Swayne's hartebeest, however, appears to be safe for the time being, as in Somalia there are some 2,000–3,000 in several well-protected herds.

EASY TARGETS

The reduncines compete less directly with domestic cattle for food, but their habitats have nevertheless been severely reduced as farmland has expanded, and they too are hunted. Reedbuck have the unfortunate reputation of being one of the easiest antelope to approach and kill. They are one of the least wary, and even when a reedbuck does take flight, it usually stops within a short distance in order to look back and assess the situation, making it an easy target.

The kob is not yet endangered—in the Boma grasslands of Sudan there are nearly one million animals. However, like most antelope, it's range has been reduced. Its water-loving relative, the lechwe, however, is classified as vulnerable by the IUCN. The largest remaining population inhabits the Kafue flats in Zambia, where two dams completed in 1970 are thought to have been the cause of a halving of the population. They may have interfered with natural fluctuations of water levels in this semiaquatic habitat sufficiently enough to reduce food production and disrupt their breeding system.

The disaster predicted at the time has not yet occurred, but the population is now down to

Trevor Barrett/Bruce Coleman Ltd.

OPERATION ORYX

The probable extinction of the Arabian oryx was foreseen during the 1960s, as people all over the world began to become conscious of the fact that animal species were disappearing as a result of human activity. Attempts had been made in several Arab countries to establish captive herds, but it was as a result of an international effort, known as "Operation Oryx", that the species was saved.

Arabian oryx heads had long been prized as trophies and, as the species became rarer, such trophies became even more valuable to the hunters. In 1961 a mechanized hunting party traveled 600 miles from Qatar on the Arabian Gulf in order to raid the last known remaining wild herd in South Yemen.

Faced with such determination to acquire trophies, even if it meant wiping out the species, the Fauna Preservation Society in London decided to make plans to rescue some of the last remaining animals. In April 1962 "Operation Oryx" was launched, financed by The World Wide Fund For Nature and the Shikar Safari Club, with the result that three wild Arabian oryx were captured. They and other individuals, donated by King Saud of Saudi Arabia and the Zoological Society of London, were taken to Phoenix Zoo in the United States and this herd, known as the "world herd" of Arabian oryx, became the reservoir for a worldwide breeding program.

CONSERVATION MEASURES

● The setting up of two Bontebok National Parks, the first in 1931 and the second in 1961, has prevented the bontebok from slipping into extinction.

● Following on from the successful Operation Oryx that was launched in 1962 to save the Arabian oryx from extinction in the wild, conservationists' hopes are now directed at the Jiddat al Harasis herd. This herd is now managed by

By 1977 there were about 80 Arabian oryx held in six separate collections. Three years later there were nearly 400, and it was considered that the program had been sufficiently successful to allow the oryx to be reintroduced into their native habitat. Much thought had been given to the difficulties that captive oryx might face in the wild and so the process was carried out as slowly as possible in controlled stages.

Today there are about 110 individuals in the wild. As a precaution against the final extinction of the Arabian oryx, 300 individuals are still held in captivity in the Arabian Peninsula, and there are another 370 held elsewhere, mainly in Phoenix and San Diego zoos. The genetics of these captive populations is being carefully studied in order to counter inbreeding and create a population with a broad genetic base.

ANTELOPE IN DANGER

THIS CHART SHOWS HOW THE INTERNATIONAL UNION FOR THE CONSERVATION OF NATURE (IUCN) CLASSIFIES THE FOLLOWING SPECIES OF ANTELOPE:

NILGAI	ENDANGERED
HIROLA	RARE
LECHWE	VULNERABLE
ARABIAN ORYX	ENDANGERED
SCIMITAR ORYX	ENDANGERED
ADDAX	ENDANGERED

ENDANGERED MEANS THAT THE ANIMAL IS IN DANGER OF EXTINCTION AND ITS SURVIVAL IS UNLIKELY UNLESS STEPS ARE TAKEN TO SAVE IT.

K.W. Fink/Ardea

PRIZED AS A TROPHY, THE ARABIAN ORYX WAS HUNTED TO THE BRINK OF EXTINCTION.

the Harasis tribe, who have sworn to protect these animals in the land where they formerly roamed free.

● Meanwhile, controlled international breeding programs are being carried out wherever the Arabian oryx is held in captivity, with a view to reintroducing genetically strong animals into the wild.

● A wildlife reserve has been set up in Niger to help save the addax.

50,000 in this area, while other populations have declined drastically as a result of uncontrolled hunting and loss of habitat. The Nile lechwe, of which there are just 30,000–40,000 individuals left in a small, swampy region of the Nile valley, is also easy prey for hunters and it, too, could be vulnerable to water development projects.

DRIED-UP HABITATS

The inhabitants of arid regions are even more vulnerable to disruption of their delicately balanced habitats. Any increase in desertification reduces their food supply, and the open country they inhabit affords no cover to protect them from hunters. The Arabian oryx is one of the most notorious cases of a wild species having been virtually wiped out (see Endangered Species).

The scimitar oryx has also suffered at the hands of man and is now classified as endangered. It has long been hunted, and, as early as 1850, its range was beginning to be reduced. Increased hunting combined with a series of droughts has dramatically reduced the population in recent years. During the 1970s there were around 6,000 individuals present in the southern part of the Sahara desert. Today, the only wild animals known to exist belong to a herd in southern Chad. About 550 individuals are held in zoos.

The addax, despite being the most desert-adapted of all these species, is also under threat. Being a large antelope, it cannot run away very quickly and is therefore easy prey for hunters. Its meat and skin are prized by natives of the region who use the tough leather for making the soles of shoes and sandals. As well as being ruthlessly hunted for its meat and skin it has been affected by drought and even by tourists, some of whom chase addax in motorized vehicles until the animals are exhausted.

The roan and sable antelope still occur in relatively large numbers over wide areas, but populations are declining as a result of habitat deterioration, agricultural encroachment, and illegal hunting. Their situation is not helped by the fact that in some places they are deliberately slaughtered as part of a program for controlling tsetse fly.

One other hippotragine, the bluebuck—not to be confused with the nilgai or "blue buck" (Boselaphus tragocamelus)—has the dubious distinction of having been the first African mammal to have been wiped out by white people (see right).

FATE OF THE SPIRAL-HORNS

Hunting and habitat destruction are worldwide problems and few species are immune, particularly among large mammals. In Africa, as elsewhere, woodland and rain forest are constantly being cleared to create more land for farming. The mountain nyala, which has always been restricted to a small highland region of Ethiopia since it was first discovered in 1908, has declined noticeably over the years. The current population is around 3,000—less than half the population that existed in the 1960s. Similarly, the greater kudu,

ALONGSIDE MAN

WIPED OUT BY THE WHITE MAN

Standing about 40 in (100 cm) at the shoulder and with a distinctive blue-gray coat, the bluebuck (*Hippotragus leucophaeus*) once lived and grazed in the wooded savanna of South Africa. Although there is evidence to suggest that this species was declining due to natural causes, its demise was hastened by man, initially by the introduction of domestic sheep into its habitat in about A.D. 400. By the time the white settlers arrived in Africa in the 18th century, its range had been reduced to a small coastal region in South Africa. They offered a challenge to the huntsman, which resulted in the last individuals being killed in about 1800, long before any thought was given to the idea of conservation. All that remains of this species is one stuffed specimen in the museum of Leiden, Germany, and a few skulls and other remains in various university museums.

Hardier than their cattle cousins, herds of eland are now being farmed in some areas. They are used as draft animals, or kept for dairy or meat production.

which is prized by hunters for its horns and meat and is also killed because it is said to damage crops, now has a considerably reduced range due to loss of habitat. Populations of the lesser kudu, too, have been greatly reduced over the years, and the population believed to have existed in the Arabian Peninsula was probably wiped out by hunters. Eland, too, have disappeared over much of their range, and the giant eland is classified by the IUCN as endangered. ∎

Nigel Dennis/NHPA

INTO THE FUTURE

The fortunes of the different species of grazing and spiral-horned antelope have been, and continue to be somewhat mixed. On the one hand, species such as impala and blue wildebeest seem secure for the time being. They are present in large numbers and their savanna environment is not especially threatened. In contrast, the future of species such as the hirola and the lechwe is less assured, and the future of the two species of oryx and the addax remains questionable in spite of the efforts made to save them.

The sad fact is that the factors that have caused these species to decline in numbers continue to operate. As in the case of many large mammals, the main factors are hunting, both legal and illegal, loss of habitat due to encroachment by agriculture, and fencing-in of land that prevents nomadic species from gaining access to

PREDICTION

A WELCOME SIDE EFFECT FOR WILDEBEESTS

While the African savanna still exists, the blue wildebeest will continue to survive. Recent warfare against the disease rinderpest in cattle, a disease that normally kills 8 percent of young wildebeests each year, has caused an increase in wildebeest populations.

water. These factors may also be aggravated by disasters such as civil war or drought.

Such secondary factors by themselves do not necessarily have a lasting effect upon wild animals, but when they add to the difficulties of a species that is already under pressure, the result can be disastrous.

There is, therefore, no room for complacency. Many of the world's species of large mammals are declining in numbers, either slowly or rapidly, and the majority of these antelope are no exception. Within the near future many of these species are likely to be reduced to a number of small populations of 100 individuals or less confined to relatively small areas.

In such circumstances populations will be at risk of becoming extinct as a result of chance events. Such risks can be reduced by careful management, but it seems very possible that the populations of some species will be reduced to a few zoo specimens or even disappear forever. ∎

Joanne Cowne

HOPE FOR THE ADDAX

The last remaining strongholds of the addax are in Chad and Niger. However, although there is a reserve in Chad, the population of addax has been decimated as a result of civil war; soldiers in the desert need food and have the means to kill.

In Niger, on the other hand, the situation is more hopeful. The government has set aside over 19 million acres as a wildlife reserve, and, together with funds and expert help from The World Wide Fund for Nature (WWF) and the IUCN, this may help to save the addax from extinction.

CATTLE OF THE FUTURE

There are few wild mammals that are sufficiently docile to tame, but one of these is the eland, and there is evidence from rock paintings that bushmen in the Kalahari desert may have domesticated this species in the past. More recently, several herds of common eland have been established with a view to their domestication. At Askanija Nova in the former USSR there is a herd kept for dairy production—eland milk is said to have three times the fat content and twice the protein content of the milk from a dairy cow. At Natal in South Africa another herd has been developed for use as draft animals. And elsewhere there are herds for meat production—eland can thrive on poorer grazing than domestic cattle and hence may be useful on marginal land.

ARMADILLOS

Norbert Wu/Planet Earth Pictures

Armadillos and pangolins were once thought to be related. They are both edentates, which means "lacking teeth," but they are now classified in two separate orders: the New World Edentata (armadillos, sloths, and anteaters) and the Old World Pholidota (pangolins).

ORDER
Edentata
(armadillos, sloths, and anteaters)

FAMILY
Dasypodidae
(armadillos)

EIGHT GENERA

TWENTY SPECIES

ORDER
Pholidota
(pangolins)

FAMILY
Manidae
(pangolins)

ONE GENUS

SEVEN SPECIES

ARMED TO THE HILT

CONTINENTS APART, BUT SHARING SIMILAR WORLDS, THESE BIZARRE-LOOKING, ARMORED, INSECT-EATING MAMMALS DISPLAY MANY SIMILAR TRAITS AND A COMMON ANCESTRY

Both armadillos and pangolins are remarkable for their bony suits of armor, which act as natural barriers against predators. Ironically, however, this means of protection has been one of the chief reasons for their exploitation by humans.

STRANGE BUT TRUE

Although armadillos were well known to the native Indian peoples of tropical America, who had various names to describe the different species, the word *armadillo* was coined by the Spanish conquistadors who colonized parts of Mexico and Central and South America in the 16th century. To see these armor-plated, prehistoric-looking creatures scuttling away and trying to bury themselves in sandy soil must have amazed and amused the Spaniards. The word *armadillo* derives from the Spanish word *armado*, meaning "one who is armed."

81

On the continents of Africa and Asia, the superficially similar pangolins must also have been a source of wonder to their European dis- coverers. Skins of these strange, scaled beasts were brought back to western Europe in Roman times, and 16th-century scientists were aware of the existence of armored creatures from Africa and Asia. However, pangolins caused so much confusion that it was a further two centuries before a European zoologist, Frenchman Baron Cuvier, decided that they were mammals and not reptiles. The word *pangolin* itself is from the Malay *peng-goling*, meaning "the roller," from the animal's habit of curling into a ball. The scales form a shield that only the larger cats and hye- nas with their bone-crushing jaws can penetrate.

SIMILAR TRAITS

Armadillos and pangolins live mainly in grasslands and tropical forests. Here, they are protected from most predators by their strong armor plating. Their heavily clawed forelimbs enable them to burrow out living quarters, and, in the case of pangolins, are used with their flexible tails to climb trees. In fact, two African species of

Daniel J. Cox/Oxford Scientific Films

Gerald Cubitt/Bruce Coleman Ltd.

A common long-nosed armadillo (right) *is the most widespread of the twenty armadillo species.*

CLOSE RELATIVES?

Armadillos and pangolins, although originally thought to be closely related, are now considered to belong to different orders of mammals. Armadillos belong to the order Edentata (EE-den-tah-ta), meaning "lacking teeth," along with anteaters and sloths, while pangolins are classified in a separate order of their own, the Pholidota (FOAL-ee-doe-ta), meaning "scaled animals."

Both groups of animals share adaptations for a diet of insects, such as long, sticky tongues and powerful, clawed forefeet for digging for prey; however, these are thought to be the result of convergent evolution (the development of similar external body shape and features in unrelated animals as each adapts to a similar way of life). There is still some disagreement about the evolution of armadillos. Some authorities believe that fossil edentates (armadillos, sloths, and anteaters) are more closely related to pangolins than to the present-day edentates.

pangolins—the small-scaled tree pangolin and the long-tailed pangolin—are almost exclusively arboreal (tree-living) and are very dependent on their prehensile tails, which they can curl tightly around branches for support and stability when they are high in the forest canopy. The long-tailed pangolin is particularly restricted to the upper layers of the forest, and its forty-six or forty-seven tail vertebrae—more than in any other living mammal—equip it well for its precarious existence.

TOOTHLESS, NOT USELESS!
Pangolins use their acute sense of smell to seek out ants and termites, then use their powerful forelimbs to crack open anthills and termite mounds. They probe for and lap up their diminutive prey with their long, saliva-covered tongues. In contrast to pangolins, with their highly restricted diet, most species of armadillos eat a variety of food, including plant tubers, fallen fruits, and carrion, as well as insects.

Both groups of animals have evolved to survive on these restricted diets. They have very few teeth or none at all, long straplike tongues for scooping up prey, and thick, muscular stomach walls for grinding up tough-shelled insects.

The Indian pangolin and the other two Asian species (inset) *are mainly terrestrial, but they can climb well.*

Although some species of armadillos lack teeth completely, most do, in fact, have small, cylindrical, peglike teeth that lack enamel. However, these teeth are of little help in chewing food. Pangolins have no teeth whatsoever.

RANGE OF SPECIES

Four species of pangolins inhabit the African rain forests, and a further three species occur in forest habitats in Asia, although nowhere are the Asian pangolins abundant.

Armadillos, on the other hand, are confined to the New World, with a range extending from South America, up through Central America, and into the southern states of the United States. A total of twenty species of armadillos range the forests and grasslands, and although many species, such as the giant armadillo of South America, have declined and are now endangered, at least one—the long-nosed armadillo—has recently expanded its range and is found throughout the southern United States.

One of the most likely theories for this expansion of range over the last hundred years is that it may be partly due to a general warming of the climate (global warming) during this period. ■

YELLOW ARMADILLO

Euphractus sexcintus
(you-FRAK-tuss sex-SINK-tuss)

The yellow (or six-banded) armadillo was, until recently, classified with the three species of fairy armadillos and the pichi. As with these species, the number of bands of armor actually varies from six to eight; and, like them, its underparts are covered with a layer of coarse hair, while bristly hairs sprout between the armor plates on the animal's back.

OTHER SPECIES
PICHI, FAIRY, GIANT, LONG-NOSED, NAKED-TAILED, HAIRY, AND THREE-BANDED ARMADILLOS

ⒶNCESTORS

LUMBERING GIANTS

The ancestors of today's edentates were much more numerous (in terms of the number of species) and were much larger. Elephant-sized giant sloths roamed the land, along with *Glyptodon*, a giant armadillo with a body length of 16.5 ft (5 m) and a rigid 10 ft (3 m) shell, and its close relative the *Doedicurus (below)*, which had a massive tail with the tip armored like a medieval mace. Although these lumbering giants were mentioned in Native American legends, only the smaller tree sloths, anteaters, and armadillos persisted to the present day.

B/W Illustrations Ruth Grewcock

ANTEATERS

THE EDENTATES' FAMILY TREE

The classification of armadillos and pangolins has vexed zoologists for years. One problem is that no single set of structural features occurs consistently throughout the order Edentata. These differences relate to the development of limbs, feet, shoulder blades, and skull and the development of large, powerful claws, among other features.

OTHER SPECIES
AFRICAN
GIANT PANGOLIN, SMALL-SCALED TREE PANGOLIN, LONG-TAILED PANGOLIN

ASIAN
INDIAN PANGOLIN, CHINESE PANGOLIN, MALAYAN PANGOLIN

CAPE PANGOLIN
Manis temminckii
(MAN-iss te-MIN-kee)

One of four species of African pangolins: like the largest species, the giant pangolin, the Cape pangolin is found mainly on the ground in savanna and open woodland and spends most of the day asleep in a burrow. But unlike its relative, it does not dig its own burrow, preferring to adapt a termite mound or take over an abandoned aardvark burrow.

SLOTHS

(A)NCESTORS

THE EARLIEST PANGOLIN

The evolutionary history of pangolins is far more fragmented than that of their New World counterparts—sloths, anteaters, and armadillos. The much poorer fossil record shows that ancestors of today's pangolins originally occurred in North Africa and Europe, and it is likely that pangolins are more closely related to aardvarks than armadillos.

The earliest known pangolin is *Eomanis waldi (below)*, a small armored pangolin from the Eocene epoch (55–38 million years ago). This direct ancestor of the living African and Asian pangolins has been remarkably well preserved, even down to its characteristic scaly covering resembling a pine cone. The stomach contents of *Eomanis* are intact and show that its diet included vegetable matter as well as insects.

Color illustrations Evi Antoniou

EDENTATES

ANATOMY: THE ARMADILLO

The smallest armadillo is the lesser fairy armadillo (above left), which has a total length of 6–7 in (15–18 cm); the largest is the giant armadillo (above center) measuring up to 5 ft (1.5 m). The giant pangolin (above right) from Africa can attain a comparable total body length.

THE EARS

are quite large and prominent. Compared with its acute sense of smell, the armadillo's hearing is poorly developed.

THE EYES

are relatively small with poor vision. Thick lids protect the eyes from bites of ants and termites.

PANGOLIN SCALES

The pangolin has sharp, overlapping scales (left), which are movable and vary in color from yellowish to dark brown. The horn-and-bone body armor of the armadillo (below) is made up of bands or plates connected, or surrounded, by flexible skin.

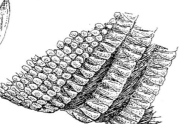

ARMADILLO SCALES

THE SNOUT

is well developed and provides armadillos and pangolins with an acute sense of smell.

X-RAY

snout

teeth

eye cavity

ARMADILLO SKULL
The armadillo's skull is elongate and flattened, with a slim mandible (jawbone) and nearly cylindrical, peglike teeth. The skull provides a casing for the long tongue, which has a more important role to play in feeding than do the teeth.

PANGOLIN SKULL
The pangolin has a conical skull, devoid of teeth or chewing muscles. Its slender jawbones and long, thin, delicate mouthparts are an adaptation to a diet of ants and termites and act as a casing for the long, viscous tongue.

conical skull

slender bottom jaw

X-ray illustrations Elisabeth Smith/Scales illustrations Ruth Grewcock

FEET

All the pangolin's limbs have five clawed feet. The three middle claws on the forefeet (top right) are long and curved for digging. The forefeet of the armadillo (bottom right) have three, four, or five digits (equivalent to fingers) with powerful, curved claws for digging, and the back feet have five digits (equivalent to toes) with claws.

PANGOLIN

ARMADILLO

FACT FILE

COMMON ARMADILLO

CLASSIFICATION

GENUS: *DASYPUS*

SPECIES: *NOVEMCINCTUS*

SIZE

HEAD–BODY LENGTH: 9–23 IN (23–58.4 CM)

TAIL LENGTH: 5–19 IN (12.5–48 CM)

WEIGHT: 2–22 LB (0.9–10 KG)

COLORATION

THE BODY IS MOTTLED BROWNISH AND YELLOWISH WHITE. PALE YELLOWISH HAIRS ARE THINLY SCATTERED ON THE UNDERPARTS, BUT HAIRS ARE LACKING ON THE UPPERPARTS

FEATURES

BROAD, LOW BODY

SHORT LEGS

BANDS OF HORN-AND-BONE BODY ARMOR CONNECTED BY FLEXIBLE SKIN

USUALLY EIGHT MOVABLE BANDS IN NORTHERN AND SOUTHERN PARTS OF RANGE, NINE MOVABLE BANDS IN CENTRAL PART OF RANGE (NORTHERN SOUTH AMERICA)

LONG, POINTED SNOUT

POWERFUL, CURVED CLAWS

GIVES BIRTH TO USUALLY FOUR OFFSPRING

THE SCALES

of the armadillo's armor grow from the skin and are composed of strong bony plates (scutes) overlaid by horn.

THE TAIL

is used to assist the armadillo in burrowing, which it does rapidly when faced with danger.

THE FEET

are powerful and clawed for ripping open anthills and termite mounds and digging earth from burrows.

PANGOLIN SKELETON

From its long, toothless snout, the pangolin's body tapers into a long tail, which it uses for climbing.

teeth

clawed feet

ARMADILLO SKELETON

The forelimbs and hind limbs are about equal in size, with large, curved claws for ripping into termite mounds.

long, toothless snout

long tail

clawed digits; middle claw long and curved

SCALY SPECIALISTS

THESE "WALKING ARTICHOKES" POSSESS SOME CHARACTERISTICS THAT ARE UNIQUE AMONG ANIMALS. EXPERT DIGGERS, THEY ARE ALSO SINGLEMINDED IN THE PURSUIT OF THEIR CRUNCHY, CRAWLING PREY

 At night, pangolins rove the forest floor in search of termite mounds and anthills. The slow and deliberate gait is a result of the animal's walking on the sides of its forefeet (in effect, on its knuckles) to protect the long claws, which are turned inward. A pangolin can also rear up on its hind legs and walk upright, the long tail stretched out to help to the animal balance. This posture is adopted when an individual needs to raise itself up to rip open a termite mound.

Generally timid by nature, pangolins initially freeze (stand motionless) when they sense danger, and then, if further interfered with, they will roll into a tight ball as a defense mechanism. When this happens they are almost impossible to unfurl, and, as an additional defense, the sharp-edged scales erect to further deter would-be predators. If an attempt is made to unroll it, the pangolin slides its tail in a sideways movement over the scales of its back while remaining in the ball position. Any hands or fingers trapped between the edges of the scaly tail and the scales on the back can be severely lacerated. Pangolins also adopt this curled ball posture when sleeping.

Pangolins also need protection from their food source. Termites and ants can bite painfully when their colony is being disturbed, but pangolins are equal to this. Facial parts are protected: eyes are thickly lidded, nostrils and ears can be closed, and the forehead is coated with tough skin. Adults, pupae, larvae, and eggs of ants are all eaten. Indeed, it seems as if a pangolin will eat little else, being highly selective in its choice of food. Because the pangolin has no teeth, ants and termites that are ingested must be crushed in the stomach. Muscular stomach walls are essential to this process, as are the tiny pebbles that are taken in with the ants and termites as the animal feeds.

Although armadillos can be found in forest areas, they prefer the open grassland areas of pampas (the vast, treeless plains of South America). Like the pangolins, however, they tend to be solitary; but they may also travel in pairs or in small bands, seeking out food, which in the case of armadillos will include invertebrates, carrion, and plant materials, as well as insects. Some species, such as the giant armadillo, are strictly nocturnal, while others are active by day; most, however, have a combination of the two lifestyles.

SPEEDY BURROWERS

All armadillos are powerful diggers, whether in search of food, in the construction of sleeping and breeding dens, or in keeping away from predators.

Naked-tailed armadillos (above) *live in the forests and savannas of Central and South America.*

Nick Gordon/Survival Anglia

Jany Sauvanet/NHPA

BREATHLESS

The armadillo's digging power is almost legendary, and its reputation is boosted even further by an ability to hold its breath while digging. This helps to prevent dirt particles from blocking the windpipe.

Common long-nosed armadillos have been known to hold their breath for up to six minutes while digging. Armadillos possess wide bronchi (the minor air passages branching from the two main forks of the windpipe) and other wide air passages. These function as air reservoirs, meaning that the animals do not have to stop digging activities to draw breath. This makes both hunting for food items and burrowing to escape predators more efficient.

Most species live in deep underground burrows when not actively foraging. A network of tunnels may be dug out with astonishing rapidity; the forelimbs loosen the soil, which is then kicked away with the hind limbs. When looking for food, a hairy armadillo will use another tactic: it can apparently drill conical holes in the ground with its snout. After inserting the snout, it rotates its body so that a hole is literally drilled out. It can hold its breath under such circumstances for up to four minutes.

Home ranges may include several den sites. In Florida, long-nosed armadillos have been known to use up to twelve different sites. These are usually used by a single individual on different nights. The nesting den of the large hairy armadillo may contain a bed of leaves, which the female pulls under her body and then pushes into the burrow with her hind legs. If the owner of such a nest is disturbed, she will emerge from the depths of the burrow and growl at the intruder.

Although armadillos are also covered in protective plates, the initial reaction of most species under threat is either to run or to burrow. Two species, the lesser and greater fairy armadillos, are able to block their burrows by wedging their armor-plated hindquarters up against the burrow entrance while remaining inside the burrow, facing into it. Only two species of three-banded armadillos do not burrow, since they are able to roll themselves into completely enclosed balls. ■

The long-tailed pangolin stays mainly in the branches, where it searches for insect nests.

HABITATS

Pangolins mainly inhabit the tropical and sub-tropical rain forests of Africa and Asia. Some species of armadillos live in the tropical forests of South and Central America and swampy forests of the southern United States, but they are not tied to forests in the same way as, for example, the African tree-pangolin is. Most armadillo species live in open grassland.

Tropical rain forests are characterized by tall trees, which spread their sun-seeking crown branches to form a canopy, like a vast green ceiling. There will also be some huge trees, projecting out of the canopy to heights of almost 200 ft (60 m) above ground; their supportive buttress roots may extend for 12 ft (4 m) up the trunk. Lianas (woody vines) commonly hang from these large trees, which may also have strangling figs and other tree-living plants, such as orchids, bromeliads, and pitcher plants, on their higher branches. The ground vegetation may be sparse: Little light penetrates to the forest floor, except where a giant tree has died and crashed to the ground, allowing light through and ground-living plant species to flourish before trees once again occupy this space. Annual rainfall may be in the region of 60–140 in (1,500–3,000 mm), leaving forest soils moist.

In the rain forests of tropical west Africa and southeast Asia, termites swarm along the branches in the thousands. Some species actually build their nests high in the trees, grazing on the

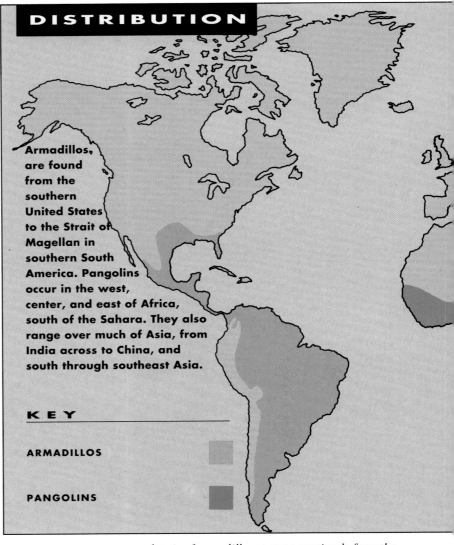

DISTRIBUTION

Armadillos, are found from the southern United States to the Strait of Magellan in southern South America. Pangolins occur in the west, center, and east of Africa, south of the Sahara. They also range over much of Asia, from India across to China, and south through southeast Asia.

KEY

ARMADILLOS

PANGOLINS

A pair of armadillos venture cautiously from the den—their only place of refuge against enemies.

lichens that sprout from the moist tree bark. The termites fall prey to tree pangolins, which patrol the branches by night.

SAVANNA DWELLERS
Many species of armadillos, and several of the pangolin species, live in savanna grassland habitats. Savannas are found around the world, mainly in Africa and South America, but there are also smaller areas in Australia and Madagascar.

These open, parklike, tropical and subtropical grasslands have scattered trees and shrubs, as well as a distinct dry season. Although many of the trees are deciduous, shedding their leaves during the dry season, the African savannas include numerous thorny acacias, whose very small leaves enable them to avoid losing too much water even though they remain on the trees all

Jeff Foott/Survival Anglia

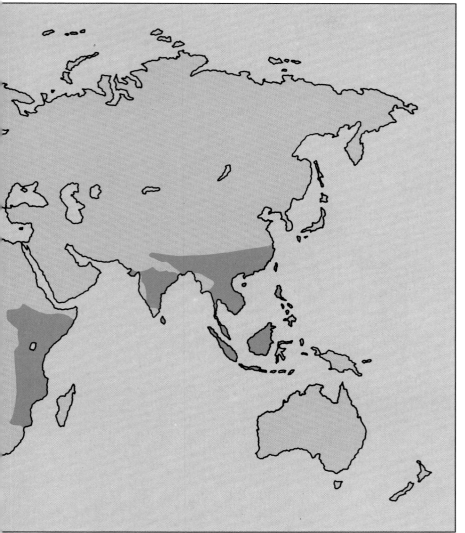

THE TERMITE MOUND

Termites are found throughout the tropics and also in the temperate zones of the world. There are more than 1,900 species of termites, which, although resembling ants, belong to a different order.

Termites live socially in mounds that they construct by chewing cellulose (a plant tissue). These mounds may be many decades old and grow taller than a human.

Each colony has three types of termites: workers to build and expand the mound, soldiers to protect the mound, and reproducers—a king and queen. The queen may live for 60 to 70 years and may produce up to 36,000 eggs per day over a 50-year period. Alates (winged termites) develop from some of these eggs when the colony is well established and on warm days take wing to establish new colonies.

Armadillos and pangolins have been known to be very choosy about which species of termites they will eat, actually steering clear of some termite mounds while actively seeking out their preferred species. The Cape pangolin, for example, which prefers juvenile ants and termites, is able to select the correct prey species simply by sniffing at the mounds.

Pangolins are superbly armored. They have little trouble devastating termite mounds.

year round. Other types of trees found in the African savanna include groups of date palms and the solitary baobab tree. This native African tree, with its swollen, barrel-like trunk, snaking branches, and gourdlike fruits, is a familiar sight in the African grasslands. The burning of these grasslands is a very common practice in Africa, so much so that only plant species that can withstand regular fires are able to survive there.

The Cape pangolin is one of the least well known of the larger African mammals; although occurring over most of southern and eastern Africa, it is generally uncommon throughout this range. It occurs in a range of savanna habitats, including both arid, scrubby areas and areas of higher rainfall in various types of savanna woodland. Cape pangolins do not occur in forest or desert areas. An important daily requirement for

Jan & Des Bartlett/Survival Anglia

this pangolin is shelter during the daylight hours when it is inactive—rock crevices, holes in the ground, or ground vegetation will be used.

PANGOLINS AT HOME

The giant pangolin lives in savanna and forested regions from west Africa east to the shores of Lake Victoria. Unlike the Cape pangolin, it cannot abide arid areas and depends on both a high rainfall and an abundance of termites for its survival. Within its home range, the giant pangolin often wears down tracks that lead to rivers and swamps, which suggests that it drinks regularly. In such habitats, termites are easily found—some species feed on the grasslands where livestock graze, while others prefer the forested valleys.

The giant pangolin's ground burrows vary greatly in their extent. In some cases, tunnels may be dug some 16 ft (5 m) below ground and up to a length of 130 ft (40 m), while other burrows are little more than scrapes, barely large enough to accommodate the animal's body. In the more extensive burrows, the giant pangolin enlarges a central chamber for its main refuge, from which several tunnels may radiate.

Tree pangolins are widespread throughout the lowland forests of Africa. Like its relatives, it

Jan & Des Bartlett/Survival Anglia

FOCUS ON

ETOSHA NATIONAL PARK

This prestigious national park in Namibia was named after Etosha Pan, "the great white place of dry water," which lies near the eastern end of the park. The pan is an extensive, flat depression, which is parched and barren during the dry months, but partially floods during the November–April rainy season. The brackish water that partly fills the pan is too salty for consumption; instead, it supports blooms of blue-green algae and provides an ideal breeding site for up to one million pairs of flamingoes.

The springs and rain-fed pools fringing the pan provide water for mammals, attracting them in hordes in the dry season. Plains zebra, wildebeest, hartebeest, gemsbok, kudu, springbok, giraffe, and many other species congregate there; in turn, these herds attract predators and scavengers such as leopards, lions, hyenas, and cheetahs.

The open savanna grasslands are dotted with wild fig trees, date palms, and tambouti, a deciduous hardwood tree. In more arid parts of the park, thorn-shrub savanna is more common.

TEMPERATURE AND RAINFALL

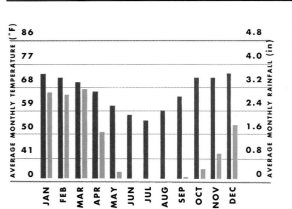

■ **TEMPERATURE**

▨ **RAINFALL**

The figures given are for Windhoek, the capital city that lies in central Namibia. The north is moister, but this is due mainly to river drainage rather than to a higher rainfall. The average annual rainfall for the north is around 20 in (500 mm).

feeds on termites, but also on ants; these insects favor the type of forest that has been partially cleared by humans, then allowed to regenerate. The pangolin finds resting sites in hollow trees or in the sockets left in trunks by ripped-out branches. Often, such places of refuge are 50 ft (15 m) or more above ground.

In these forests, the tree pangolin is in its element. Aided by its prehensile tail, it clambers with care through the twisting lianas and branches and shuffles up broad trunks in search of prey. ■

NEIGHBORS

Lying next to South Africa, Namibia is probably most famous for the sweeping sand dunes of the dusty Namib desert; but in terms of plants and animals, it is a country of surprising richness.

MEERKAT

These sleek, burrowing carnivores are related to mongooses and live in close-knit colonies.

ELEPHANT

The African elephant is found in a range of African habitats, from semidesert to high mountain forest.

ETOSHA PAN

Etosha Pan lies in the north of Namibia, close to the Angola border. Namibia is dominated by the scrublands of the central plateau and the rolling, sandy wastes of the Namib and Kalahari. These deserts have a unique and special plant life.

ANGOLA

ETOSHA PAN

NAMIBIA

BOTSWANA

ATLANTIC OCEAN

LEOPARD

This solitary, nocturnal stalker generally hunts small and medium-sized antelopes and deer.

OSTRICH

The largest living bird, the ostrich is also flightless. Adult males may stand nearly 8 ft (2.5 m) tall.

BLACK MAMBA

This venomous snake dens in open, rocky country. A relative of the cobras, it hunts small mammals.

PEL'S FISHING OWL

Rarely found in Namibia, this species shares its range with the Cape pangolin in Zambia and Tanzania.

NILE CROCODILE

One of the most dangerous of Africa's reptiles, this crocodile lies in wait for mammals at water holes.

FOOD AND FEEDING

Armadillos and pangolins feed on a specialized small-food diet that consists of the various life stages of ants and termites. Because it is essential that they be able to deal effectively with large numbers of these small prey, both groups share adaptations for this special feeding behavior.

ARMORED BULLDOZERS

Scales or armor protect the majority of the body from the biting intentions of the insects. Instead of diligently picking their route into anthills and termite mounds, armadillos and pangolins specialize in the bulldozer approach. With its short muscular legs and strong claws, the giant armadillo burrows a sizable tunnel into the center of the mound until it reaches the heart of the colony, seemingly unconcerned by the attentions of thousands of angry soldier termites.

When foraging, an armadillo starts by using its well-developed sense of smell to locate prey. It first thrusts its snout as far as possible into the leaf litter. Then, as soon as it detects insects, it

Jeff Foott/Survival Anglia

A common long-nosed armadillo (above) *feasts on a meal of grubs, which it has located using its acute sense of smell.*

KEY FACTS

● **Giant armadillos have reportedly dug into new graves to eat corpses. Several species of armadillos eat carrion, although it is not always known whether the species concerned is present to eat flesh or to consume the insects and other creatures attracted to the carcass.**

● **Hairy armadillos have been seen killing snakes by cutting them with the hard edges of their carapaces. They then partially eat them.**

● **A common long-nosed (nine-banded) armadillo can lap up 40,000 ants at a single sitting.**

● **The stomach contents of a Malayan pangolin were found to weigh 4.4 oz (125 g), comprising approximately 200,000 ant workers and pupae. If this represents an average day's food intake, then an adult of this species eats about 73 million ants per year.**

Illustrations Kim Thompson

NEST ATTACK

African long-tailed pangolins attack a hanging nest of tree termites with their sharp-clawed forefeet. The termites are then gathered up on the long, sticky tongue.

PLOWING POWER

Armadillos are expert diggers and will quickly excavate an insect nest or rip open a termite mound using their clawed feet.

starts to excavate a conical hole, using short, alternate strokes of the forefeet. The snout is pushed farther into the soil with each thrust and is not lifted from the soil while digging is in progress. Insects such as beetle larvae may be detected at a depth of up to 5 in (12 cm) below the soil surface in this way. Once caught, the beetle grub is hastily crushed and swallowed. Then the animal continues its nose-to-the-ground plowing.

Saliva for trapping insects on the long, sticky tongue is produced by the salivary glands and stored in a special salivary reservoir or bladder.

More unusual armadillo food items have included young rabbits excavated from underground nests. Additionally, observations from San Antonio, Texas, have shown that the pulpy fruit from the black persimmon forms up to 80 percent of the diet of the common armadillo when the fruit is in season. The success of this latter species in expanding its range and colonizing new areas is due in part to its omnivorous feeding habits (it eats both animal and vegetable matter). In fact, in the southeastern United States, it has been so successful that it is regarded as a pest in some arable areas, where it causes damage to crops by digging and feeding. ■

*in*SIGHT

EATING ON HIGH

The two tree-dwelling African pangolins will come to the ground to eat termites, but they are adapted to life in the trees. The small-scaled tree pangolin forages in the lower branches of forest trees by night, while its smaller relative, the long-tailed tree pangolin, is more closely restricted to the forest canopy. Here it hunts by day to avoid confrontation with its larger relative. The muscular tail of both species has a bare spot at the tip, which is used to find suitable places on the tree's trunk or branches for the tail to grab. In order to break up nests of tree termites, tree pangolins anchor themselves in the branches using their hind limbs and prehensile tails, which they wrap around nearby branches. The claws of the forefeet are then used to enlarge the cavity leading into the nest.

SOCIAL STRUCTURE

As a rule, armadillos and pangolins are solitary creatures. Individuals do not generally display the strong territoriality seen in many other mammals, but will mark conspicuous objects, such as tree stumps, large stones, and paths, with secretions from scent glands and, in some species, urine.

Such marking probably has a dual function: first, to advertise an individual's presence, status, and sexual condition; and second, to promote loose territorial boundaries, which may be important in securing access to scarce food resources.

TERRITORIES AND DISPUTES

For armadillos, the degree of preservation of home range territories varies from species to species and between sexes. For example, the ranges of male common long-nosed (nine-banded) armadillos are up to 50 percent larger than those of the females and frequently overlap. Females of this species are, however, much likelier to maintain an exclusive home range.

At least in common long-nosed armadillos, an individual's home range (or loose territory) is maintained by use of the sense of smell, and, to a lesser degree, aggression, with the poorly developed senses of sight and hearing being of much less relevance. On meeting, adult animals sniff at each other's hindquarters and are presumably able to recognize individuals on this basis; the strong odor given off derives from the yellow, pungent secretion produced by the pair of bean-shaped anal glands. This secretion is also likely to deter predators; and in the case of pangolins,

the secretion is physically squirted at predators that try to unroll the pangolin from its protective ball shape.

Because armadillos cannot squirt their secretion at intruders, physical contact may be used to resolve territorial disputes. Kicking, chasing, and fighting, accompanied by high-pitched squeals, are the commonest methods of settling such disputes.

VIVE LA DIFFERENCE!

For pangolins, our knowledge of activity and territory size is even scantier. Research on the African tree pangolins has shown that males of these species have larger territories, are active longer during the main period of activity, and range much farther than the females.

Whereas males have territories of 35–62 acres (14–24.8 hectares), female territories only cover 7–10 acres (2.8–4 hectares); in other words, male territories are in some cases about six times larger than those of the females. Males are on average active for much longer periods during the night (two to ten hours) than females (three to four hours) and travel about a half

ANT BATH

Pangolins appear to take "ant baths" by lying in an ants' nest and allowing the insects to crawl all over them. It is thought that the formic acid that is absorbed into the pangolin's skin is essential to its health.

Color illlustrations Rachel Lockwood/Wildlife Art Agency

● Female pangolins roam around their territories following a zigzag or circular course. As a result, they cover only part of their territories, which, along with scent markings, ensures that female pangolins rarely meet other females.

● Although several species of armadillos are solitary animals, certain species will come together to feed. The six-banded armadillo will group at a carcass to feed on meat and maggots. Individuals of the same species may inhabit the same burrow. In the case of long-nosed armadillos and southern three-banded armadillos, for example, up to twelve animals have been found together in a single burrow during the cold season.

mile (800 m), compared with the average female traveling distance of a quarter mile (400 m).

Marking is as important for pangolins as it is for armadillos; marking boundaries of territories ensures that males rarely meet, whereas the scent markings of females alert males to the readiness of the females to mate. The scent produced by an individual pangolin reveals important information concerning the physiological state of that individual; hence males will be deterred from contact, particularly where the presence of an aggressive individual is detected. This ensures that sources of conflict are avoided. Indeed, aggression between male pangolins has been observed only infrequently, at which time pangolins are known to emit a hissing sound. ■

NO SQUATTERS!

A giant armadillo protects its burrow from a tayra. This weasel-like animal from South America has a tendency to borrow burrows to rest up in during the day.

ROLLING DEFENSES

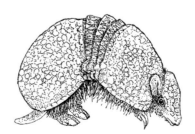

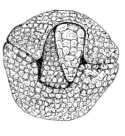

The southern three-banded armadillo and the extremely rare Brazilian three-banded armadillo are the only two species that can roll themselves into an almost impenetrable ball when faced with danger. Other species roll up to a lesser degree or will run and burrow when faced with danger.

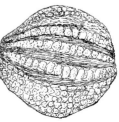

B/W illustrations Ruth Grewcock

LIFE CYCLE

The life cycles of many species of armadillos and pangolins remain sketchy. This is partly because many of the species are studied little in the wild. At least in the case of pangolins, it is also because they are notoriously difficult to keep in captivity, particularly outside the tropics, due to their very precise dietary requirements.

SECRETIVE BREEDERS

There is little information about armadillo mating behavior, although it seems likely that scent marking is important in alerting males to the presence of a sexually receptive female.

Armadillos are unusual among the majority of mammals in that they display delayed implantation. This is the process whereby the single egg, having been fertilized by the male, lies in the female's uterus for a period of time (in this case several months) before becoming embedded in the uterine wall where development can take place. This method of reproduction allows the adults to mate at a time that is convenient for them, but delays the development of the offspring, enabling the young to be born during the spring growing season when food is plentiful and the climate more amenable.

Even more unusual, several identical young of the same sex are produced from a single egg. Usually two to four young are produced in this way, but as many as twelve have been recorded.

At birth, armadillos are fully developed, having fully formed and hardened claws but, at least in some species, with the eyes and ear flaps closed (these open after three to four weeks in three-banded armadillos). When the young are at this vulnerable stage of development, they remain inside the burrow for protection and are suckled by the mother. Armadillo young also have soft, leathery skin, which soon hardens, and the young armadillos are able to walk within a few hours of

COURTSHIP

Armadillos seem to court somewhat secretly! Though little is known about armadillo breeding habits, it is thought that the female scent marks the area to alert males that she will be receptive.

STRIKING OUT

After a few weeks the young armadillo is weaned and leaves the the nest to start foraging for insects.

COMING OF AGE

Adolescent armadillos become sexually mature when they are between six and twelve months old.

birth. Captive young six-banded armadillos are known to take solid foods at one month old.

Pangolins share a not dissimilar life cycle with armadillos. The young are born in burrows, or, in the case of the arboreal species, in cavities in trees. They seem to be born at any time of the year, with a single young, rarely two, being produced.

Their scales are soft at birth but start to harden by the second day. Giant pangolins are born with their eyes open. And even though they cannot yet support their own weight, they are very

Alan Root/Survival Anglia

GROWING UP
The life of a young armadillo

Traveling by tail is the only way to go for a young African tree pangolin (above).

Illustrations Barry Croucher/Wildlife Art Agency

QUADS
Common armadillos give birth to four young of the same sex. Other species have between one and four young.

TOUGHENING UP
The soft, pink, leathery skin of a newborn armadillo soon hardens.

active: at one day old they will have scrambled to their mothers' tails where they will cling with their own prehensile tails. The young of Cape pangolins are kept folded up in the coiled body of the mother. Young pangolins grow rapidly and soon double in size and weight. Weaning of the young is thought to take place at about three months.

TAIL RIDE
Female pangolins use the base of the tail to transport the young. When carried by the mother, the young pangolin usually sits across the tail, which is held clear of the ground and clings tightly with its sharp claws. If alarmed, the mother will curl into a protective posture and the youngster will find protection under the mother's stomach, further sheltered by her tail.

The role played by the male pangolin in the rearing of the young is unclear, but both male and female have been found sharing a burrow with the offspring. ■

FROM BIRTH TO DEATH

COMMON ARMADILLO	CAPE PANGOLIN
GESTATION: 120–140 DAYS	**GESTATION:** 140 DAYS
LITTER SIZE: 4 (OF ONE SEX)	**LITTER SIZE:** 1 (SOMETIMES 2 IN ASIAN SPECIES)
BREEDING: MATING TAKES PLACE JULY–AUGUST, BUT IMPLANTATION IS DELAYED UNTIL NOVEMBER	**BREEDING:** ANY TIME OF YEAR
EYES OPEN: AT BIRTH	**WEIGHT AT BIRTH:** 10–14 OZ (280–392 G)
WEANING: A FEW WEEKS	**WEANING:** 3 MONTHS
SEXUAL MATURITY: 6–12 MONTHS	**SEXUAL MATURITY:** 2 YEARS
LONGEVITY: 12–15 YEARS IN CAPTIVITY	**LONGEVITY:** OVER 11 YEARS RECORDED IN CAPTIVITY

CHINKS IN THE ARMOR

HUNTED FOR CENTURIES FOR THEIR FLESH, AND FOR THE APPARENT MEDICINAL PROPERTIES OF THEIR UNUSUAL BODY PARTS, ARMADILLOS AND PANGOLINS ARE ALSO RUNNING SHORT OF LIVING SPACE

Armadillos have for centuries played an important role in sustaining humans. Historically, the giant ancestors of today's armadillos provided food for the early South American Indians, and the large body shells of these creatures—up to 10 ft (3 m) long—were used as roofs or tombs. It is possible that the huge *Glyptodon*—despite being the size of a small car and having armor reminiscent of an army tank—was an early casualty of human hunters. The Patagonian Indians who hunted it could have had a devastating impact on its populations, since the lumbering creatures would have had no previous experience of humans and, with no suitably defensive behavior,

must have made easy targets. Even so, it cannot have been easy for primitive hunters, armed only with spears or other basic weapons, to wipe out an entire species. However, if *Glyptodons* were driven into pits or other traps, this, combined with climatic change and other factors, may have contributed to the species's eventual extinction.

Armadillo meat was much prized by native peoples and the early explorers of South America, and today the meat of several species of armadillos is still highly valued. In Central and southern South America, the six-banded, long-nosed, and

Many species are restricted to fragile ecosystems such as rain forests and savannas (below).

Dr. Ivan Polunin/NHPA

THEN & NOW

This map shows how the common long-nosed armadillo has expanded its range in the Americas since the last century.

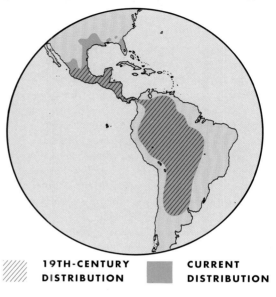

//// **19TH-CENTURY DISTRIBUTION**   ▮ **CURRENT DISTRIBUTION**

Possibly as a result of global warming, coupled with the destruction by man of its natural enemies, the common long-nosed armadillo has actually expanded its range to the north. It crossed the Rio Grande from Mexico into Texas in 1880, and it can be found today as far north as Oklahoma. As an opportunistic feeder on insect pests, it has benefited greatly by the spread of arable agriculture.

southern three-banded armadillos are hunted for their meat. These species are not seriously declining as a result of this, although the rare and geographically restricted Brazilian three-banded armadillo is under more intense pressure.

THREATENED GIANT

The giant armadillo, however, is now classified as vulnerable by the International Union for the Conservation of Nature and is listed on Appendix 1 of CITES (Convention on International Trade in Endangered Species). It has a fragmented distribution throughout much of its former range in Brazil, Peru, and elsewhere as a result of overhunting and of habitat loss through increased agricultural development and human settlement.

Despite legal protection, the Malayan pangolin is still widely hunted.

ENDANGERED SPECIES

Populations of giant armadillos are now isolated, and localized extinctions through overhunting have occurred. The opening of roads into previously undisturbed savanna and forest areas is thought to have strongly affected numbers of this species, although it is now protected through most of its range states.

Even in the most suitable habitat for the giant armadillo in the lowland forest of Surinam, South America, the estimated maximum density of this species is only about one animal in every square mile (2.6 square kilometers). Although many species of armadillos are generally more abundant than this, others, too, have been estimated to occur at very low density. For example, the greatest density estimated for the southern naked-tailed armadillo in its optimum habitat, the llanos—the savanna grasslands of the Orinoco basin of Venezuela—is about one animal per half square mile (1.3 square kilometers).

The vast expanses of savanna grassland throughout South America are undergoing huge ecological changes, primarily through the spread of agricultural practices such as cattle ranching. As the human need for land increases and more land comes under the plow, armadillo populations are threatened, with populations of the little-known fairy armadillos thought to be especially at risk. The continued provision of access roads

---

THE COMMON LONG-NOSED ARMADILLO
HAS EXPANDED NORTH INTO THE
SOUTHERN STATES OF THE UNITED STATES

---

into previously impenetrable forest areas and the continuing demand for trees for the timber industry, coupled with extensive hydroelectric dam projects, all result in major habitat destruction and a decline in armadillo populations.

LONG-NOSED SUCCESS STORY

The most successful armadillo in recent times has been the common long-nosed armadillo, which has expanded its range, in spite of this species's being hunted for food and for its armored shell in some parts of its range. This species seems able to tolerate people and their activities to some extent. It is the only species of armadillo widely considered to be a potential pest in some parts of its range, where its burrows are responsible for soil erosion and consequent damage to the foundations of buildings and to crops. Additionally this species is sometimes accused of stealing hens' eggs in some areas, although whether this is a widespread problem is open to debate.

ASIAN PANGOLINS

Asian pangolins, too, have been much hunted for food. Pangolin scales are also highly prized, especially by Chinese communities, for their alleged medicinal value; they are powdered and used as an aphrodisiac or for medicinal purposes. They are thought to possess antiseptic properties and deemed to be effective in combating fever and skin diseases, including venereal disease. Such practices have put extreme pressure on pangolin populations in some areas.

The export of dead pangolins and pangolin by-products has declined from the levels of the late 1950s and early 1960s, when over 60 tons of scales, thought to represent more than 50,000 animals, were legally exported from Sarawak to mainly Singapore over a six-year period. However, export is still extensive. Some 185,000 skins were legally exported from Asia from 1980 to 1985; 90 percent of these were exported to the United States for use in the production of leather goods, mainly boots and shoes. As a result of the decline brought about by such trade, all three Asian pangolin species are listed in CITES (SIE-tees) Appendix 2. This means that they may be imported to and traded in Europe only with a permit from the authorities in the country of origin.

However, legal protection of a species can never be fully enforced while there is still a market for its by-products. This is

CONSERVATION MEASURES

● Four species of armadillos are listed in the International Union for the Conservation of Nature's *Red Data Book* 1994 (see box on opposite page).

● The giant armadillo is listed on Appendix 1 of CITES, by which it is afforded full legal protection. Asian pangolins are listed under Appendix 2, which gives only partial protection.

proven by, for example, the continuing trades in elephant ivory and rhino horn. Materials from poached animals can be shipped with little difficulty from the country of origin because it is still easy to procure false export papers. Taiwan has recently been identified as an importer of ivory and horn, which it then distributes to Chinese medical practitioners. Like pangolin scales, rhino horn is ground up and used by the Chinese in medicinal remedies. Many of these remedies have been in use for hundreds of years, so it is not surprising that the doctors involved are reluctant to switch allegiance to modern antibiotics. Furthermore, the patients themselves are often genuinely unaware that their medicine contains products from animals that are perilously close to extinction.

Inset M. P. L. Fogden/Bruce Coleman Ltd.

ARMADILLOS & PANGOLINS IN DANGER

THE CHART BELOW SHOWS HOW THE IUCN CLASSIFIES THE STATUS OF ARMADILLOS:

GIANT ARMADILLO	VULNERABLE
BRAZILIAN THREE-BANDED ARMADILLO	ENDANGERED
GREATER PICHI CIEGO	INSUFFICIENTLY KNOWN
LESSER PICHI CIEGO	INSUFFICIENTLY KNOWN

VULNERABLE MEANS THAT THE SPECIES IS LIKELY TO BECOME ENDANGERED IN THE NEAR FUTURE IF THE CAUSAL FACTORS FOR ITS DECLINE CONTINUE TO EXIST. ENDANGERED MEANS THAT THE ANIMAL IS IN DANGER OF EXTINCTION AND ITS SURVIVAL IS UNLIKELY UNLESS STEPS ARE TAKEN TO SAVE IT. INSUFFICIENTLY KNOWN INDICATES THAT THERE IS NOT ENOUGH INFORMATION ON NUMBERS IN THE WILD FOR A MORE PRECISE CLASSIFICATION.

ORIENTAL MEDICATIONS USE BOTH THE SCALES AND BLOOD OF SPECIES SUCH AS THE CHINESE PANGOLIN.

● Many species of edentates, including armadillos, have a refuge in Manu National Park, on the eastern slopes of the Andes mountains in Peru. Manu, which was declared a biosphere reserve in 1977, includes probably the last undisturbed patch of Amazonian rain forest in Peru. The national park is home to the giant and common long-nosed armadillos, as well as three species of anteaters and two species of sloths.

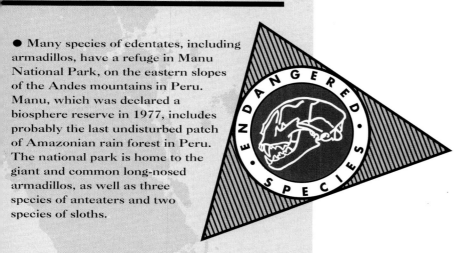

A hazard being increasingly faced by the long-nosed armadillo is the danger of being run over by road vehicles. Rather than run away from cars, the armadillo has an unfortunate habit of simply jumping up in alarm. Vehicular threat is potentially much more serious for other armadillo species, whose range is fragmented and whose numbers are declining. In areas of Central and South America where logging operations, ranching, mines, dams, and other modern developments suddenly bring high volumes of traffic to areas where vehicles were previously unknown, significant numbers of the animals may be killed.

VICTIMS OF TRADITION

The exploitation of pangolins at the hands of humans goes back for centuries. These slow-moving, rather cumbersome creatures rely on their armor for protection rather than fleetness of foot, so they can be captured by humans. Once captured, the animals are relatively defenseless. Methods of hunting include the use of snares, and in Indonesia the Malayan pangolin is hunted with dogs.

Pangolin meat is very popular with local African people, particularly the meat of the Cape pangolin, although the giant pangolin is afforded some protection because consumption of its meat is taboo for some tribes.

Pangolin scales are in great demand throughout Africa and Asia, both for ornamental decoration and for alleged medicinal and aphrodisiac properties. Indeed, the Cape pangolin is called *bwana mganga* ("master doctor") in East Africa because every part of its body is said to possess healing

ALONGSIDE MAN

LEPROSY RESEARCH

Armadillos have played a role in scientists' research into human illnesses. They can suffer from naturally acquired rabies and leprosy and may yet have a role to play in giving us a fuller understanding of these diseases.

In 1975, individuals of the common long-nosed armadillo species were found to be suffering from leprosy, with the disease recorded in 10 percent of individuals in Louisiana and from Mississippi and Texas. The relationship between leprosy in armadillos and leprosy in humans is being investigated. One aspect of this current research is the way in which leprosy is transmitted among armadillos compared to the way in which the disease spreads among humans.

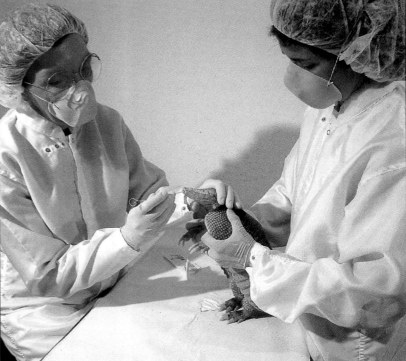

Jeff Foott/Survival Anglia

properties. The wearing of scale necklaces or bracelets is said to give the wearer great strength. Finger rings made out of scales are said to avert the evil eye, and powder from ground scales is claimed to prevent nosebleeds.

There is considerable financial incentive to those who manufacture and sell the bracelets, rings, and so on, since a single pangolin skin contains sufficient scales to make many such charms. It is difficult to dissuade people from making and using pangolin-scale charms because they are associated with deeply held beliefs.

In the Buganda region of Uganda, for example, giant pangolin scales are believed to help women. Ground up and mixed with tree bark, they make a potion that can supposedly ward off evil spirits. There is also the belief that if a pangolin scale is buried with the assistance of a soothsayer under the doorstep of a husband or lover, he will fall under its magic spell and buy his wife or lover clothes or indulge her in other ways. Pangolins are sacrificed during rainmaking ceremonies in some parts of Africa, while in others the smoke of their burning scales is believed to make cattle healthier or keep lions at bay.

In addition to being hunted for ornaments and for the medicinal or magical qualities of their scales, pangolins are vulnerable to being killed or badly injured by bush fires, and, with growing urbanization and development, increasing numbers are killed by road traffic. Such pressures,

along with habitat loss to agriculture and other developments, have caused a decline in numbers of the Cape pangolin over most of its range. Although not officially endangered, this species is listed in CITES Appendix 1, which means that trade in the animal or its parts (for example, its scales) is strictly prohibited; exceptions to this rule may be permitted only in the case of scientific zoological parks, museums, and research institutions, and in these cases strict controls are applied.

ESSENTIAL STEPS

Further protection of large areas of relatively undisturbed forest or savanna will be essential if the rarer species of armadillos and pangolins are to survive. It is particularly important to establish corridors, as well as safe havens, so that populations can intermingle and genetic diversity can be maintained. Already, many populations of the most endangered species are fragmented.

With some animals, captive breeding is an important way of sustaining numbers—as long as protected areas are set up, into which the animals can be released after they have been reared and acclimatized to life in the wild. Sadly, this is not a realistic option with armadillos and pangolins. Although they are sometimes kept in zoos, and research laboratories have experience in breeding the common long-nosed armadillo, they are not easy animals to keep, owing to their highly specialized diets, and are rarely bred in captivity. ■

A long-nosed armadillo undergoes tests and treatment for leprosy in the United States (above).

INTO THE FUTURE

Unless action is taken to reduce habitat loss and overhunting for meat and scales, several of the most threatened species of armadillos and pangolins could, in time, join their extinct ancestors. The giant armadillo, for example, has already disappeared from much of its former range in Brazil and Peru and is now classified as vulnerable in its present range.

PROTECTION PLANS

Some steps to prevent extinction have already been made, such as the provision and implementation of WWF (World Wide Fund for Nature) conservation plans to protect threatened habitats and species.

For example, one area catered to under this system is the Sinharaja Forest of Sri Lanka, the island's last remaining extensive lowland rain

PREDICTION

EXPANSION OR DECLINE?

As humans wipe out more and more of its natural enemies, such as pumas, the long-nosed armadillo should expand its range farther north in the United States. At the same time, the scarcer species of armadillos in tropical America will keep declining with accelerated habitat loss.

forest. Although not targeted specifically at pangolins, the protection of this area from encroachment of shifting agriculture and nonsustainable logging will protect the habitat of the Indian pangolin, and, it is hoped, ensure the survival of viable populations of this species.

Protected regions are also likely to play an important role in Africa and parts of South America in the future conservation of armadillo and pangolin habitats. ■

Illustration Peter Bull/Wildlife Art Agency

BACK FROM THE BRINK

The Brazilian three-banded armadillo was rediscovered in 1990 after 20 years without an authenticated sighting. Found only in the semiarid *caatinga* region of northeastern Brazil, this is one of only two species of armadillos that are able to roll themselves up into a complete ball for protection against natural predators. The other species that can do this is the southern three-banded armadillo.

The species was actually rediscovered by accident by a team of ornithologists seeking an endangered species of parrot, Lear's macaw. The field-workers discovered burned-out armadillo shells, and then five live animals for sale at a local market. These were bought and taken to a university in Belo Horizonte in southeastern Brazil. Although three of the animals died, two females survived on a diet of fruit, mealworms, and boiled eggs.

The meat of this species, which is reputed to taste like chicken, is much prized by local people. The long-nosed, six-banded, and southern three-banded armadillos are also hunted for meat throughout Central and South America. The animals are usually cooked in their own shells. In an area of low living standards, the armadillo represents a valuable source of protein for humans.

BADGERS

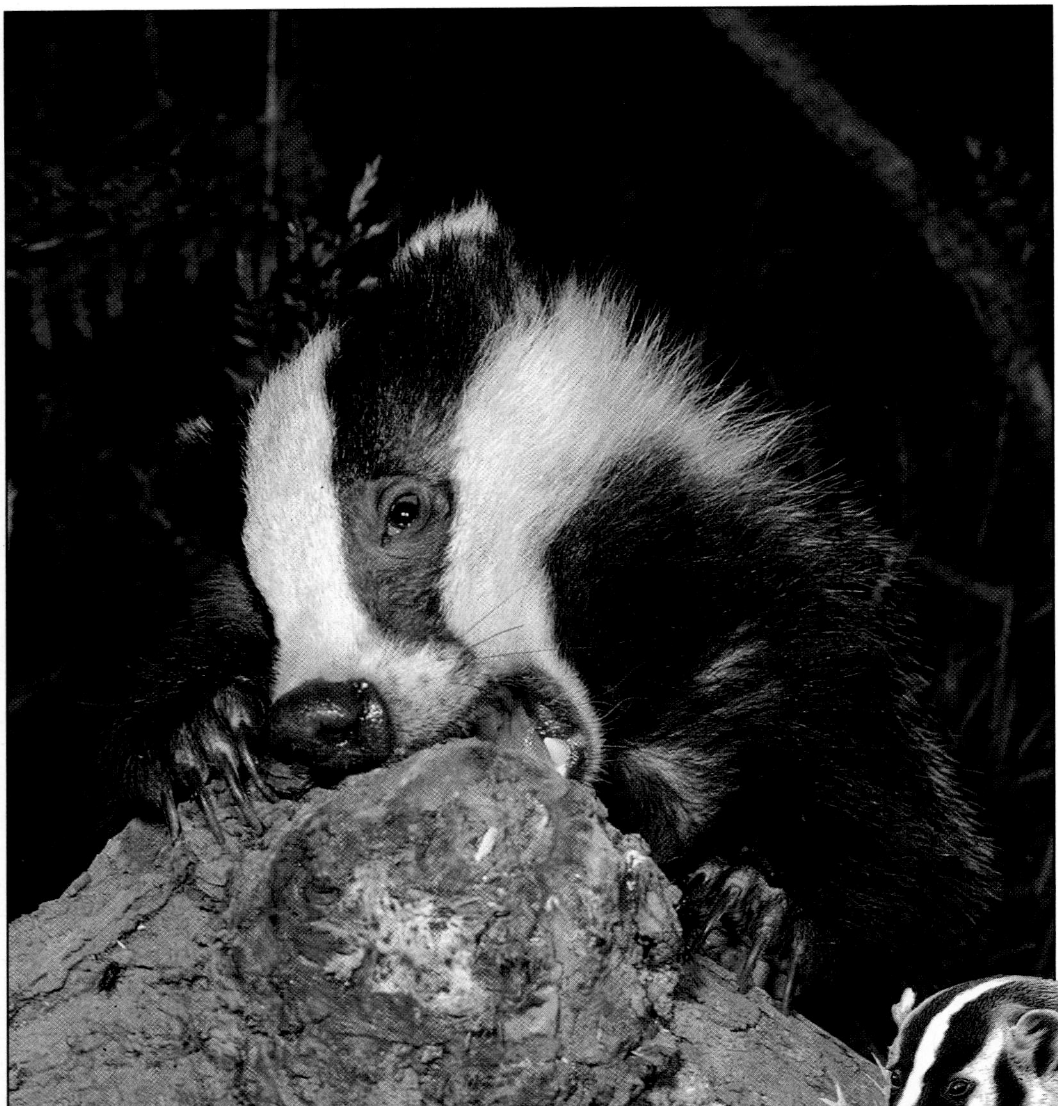

RELATIONS

The badger belongs to the family Mustelidae and the order Carnivora. Other members of this family include:

WEASELS

SKUNKS

OTTERS

ERMINE

STONE MARTEN

WOLVERINE

FERRETS

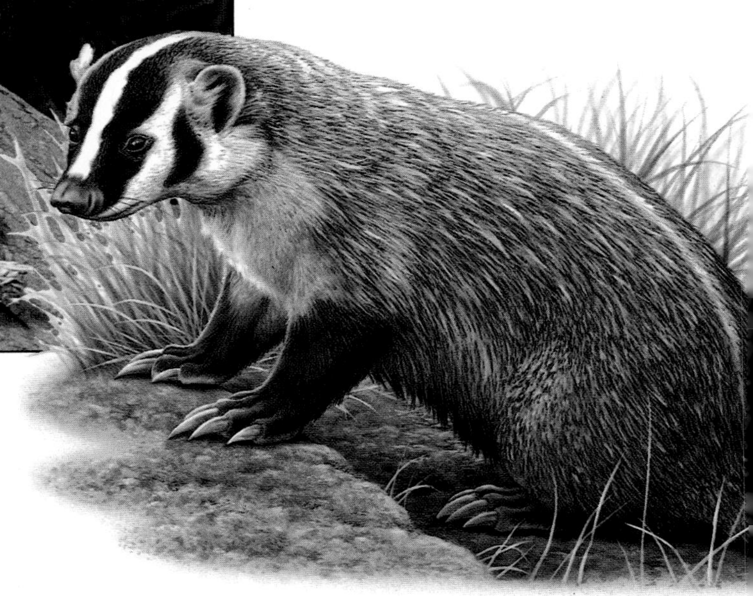

Hans Reinhard/Tony Stone Worldwide

STRIPED SENTINELS

ON BRIGHT MOONLIT NIGHTS IN EARLY SUMMER, IN WOODLANDS ALL OVER EUROPE, THE DISTINCTIVE STRIPY FACES OF EUROPEAN BADGERS MAY BE SEEN EMERGING FROM THEIR COMPLEX, SUBTERRANEAN SETTS

Usually the first badger to emerge from the safety of the sett is a mature female. Pausing at the entrance she sniffs the air to insure no danger lurks nearby. Then, before setting off on her nightly search for food, she signals to the others below that all is clear. After indulging in a lengthy grooming session, she shuffles off into the night, moving at a clumsy trot and stopping frequently to snuffle as she roots in the undergrowth.

The European badger has the widest range of all the badger species, of which there are nine across the western and central United States, southern Africa, and much of Europe, Asia, and southeast Asia. Eight are known as true badgers; the honey badger, or ratel, is placed in its own subfamily. Although the ratel is similar in behavior, there are notable differences in its dentition.

Although badgers have a highly variable diet, they are classified as carnivores, and belong to the

Ratels making a daytime appearance in Zimbabwe (below). *These badgers are more usually nocturnal.*

Nick Greaves/Planet Earth Pictures

A young European badger (right) *peers out cautiously before leaving the neighborhood of its sett.*

same family as weasels, skunks, and otters, known as the mustelids. The first carnivores to appear on earth did so during the Paleocene epoch, about 60 million years ago, and were known as the miacids. Among the best known of these was *Miacis*—an animal similar to the modern pine marten (a close relative of the weasel), which is thought to have lived in the trees of the tropical swamp forests of the time.

EVOLUTION OF THE MUSTELIDS

Mustelids evolved from the miacids, appearing during the early Miocene epoch, which began 25 million years ago. The earliest known representative was a fast-swimming animal known as Potamotherium, an otterlike animal abundant in the freshwater lakes of central France. In the Pliocene epoch, following the Miocene and beginning some 15 million years later, a mustelid from the genus *Melododon* lived in China, and it is from this species that today's European badger is thought to have evolved. The earliest fossils of the European badger have been dated from 2 million years ago, and it is known that Europe was inhabited by badgers similar in appearance to today's species from about this time. Remains in Britain go back only about 250,000 years.

All badgers are low, squat animals with short, sturdy legs, a robust, long body, a thick neck, and a relatively small head. They have a long snout, which they use for rooting in undergrowth, and

Richard Packwood/Oxford Scientific Films

impressive claws, particularly on the forefeet; those on the hind feet tend to be much shorter. All are characterized by striking pale and dark markings, although these vary both in pattern and intensity according to the species. The markings are thought to act as a warning to other animals to leave these usually peaceable animals alone.

The European badger grows the largest and heaviest. Its face is striped black and white—a broad white stripe running down the center from the forehead to the nose. Black or dark gray stripes run on either side of this extending from the snout to the ear, enclosing the eye, and are bordered by another white stripe on each cheek extending back along the neck. The small, rounded ears are ringed with white. The upper body is covered with dark gray, grizzled hair that tends to be darker underneath and on the legs.

THE WORD *BADGER* MAY DERIVE FROM THE WORD *BADGE*, DESCRIBING THE BOLD FACIAL MARKINGS

The American badger has an unmistakable flattened body with longer, shaggier hair than the European badger. This hair may be brownish or grayish. It has a white stripe extending from the shoulder down the middle of the face to the snout and white patches on either cheek. Its small ears may have white edges. The short legs look almost bowed and its forefeet are partially webbed.

The coat of the honey badger is quite different. It has a pale "cape" over the top of its head extending along its back to the tail and halfway down the sides of the body. This contrasts sharply

American badger (above) *making a sortie from its burrow in Montana.*

James A. Rowan/ Tony Stone Worldwide

109

with the dark brown or black of the rest of the fur over the lower part of the face, body, and the legs. It has a short, bushy tail, also with paler hairs on the upper part, and this is often held upward like a brush. Its tiny ears are scarcely noticeable.

The hog badger's snout is particularly elongated and also very mobile. It lacks hair and ends in a disk, not unlike a pig's snout. This badger's coloring is similar to that of the European badger, with a broad pale stripe running down the center of the face and on either cheek extending to the neck. The ears are white, as is the tail, which looks longer but much less bushy than that of the European badger. The body is covered with yellowish, grayish or almost black hairs that are darkest underneath and on the lower legs. The legs are a little longer than in other badgers. An unusual feature of the hog badger is the pale coloring of its claws; in other species the claws are dark. In its native Asian habitat, the hog badger is sometimes known as the sand badger.

> THE HOG BADGER EARNS ITS NAME FROM ITS HIGHLY MOBILE, LONG, AND TRUNCATED SNOUT, WITH WHICH IT SNIFFS OUT FOOD ON THE FOREST FLOOR

There are two so-called stink badgers: the teledu, or Malayan stink badger, and the Palawan stink badger, both found only in Borneo, Sumatra, Java, and other isolated parts of southeast Asia. They, too, are more piglike in appearance with a long, mobile snout and a short tail. The teledu has a dark brown or black coat, uniformly colored except for a white crown and a white stripe—almost like a crest—running down the center of the back and on to the tail, not unlike the markings of a skunk. The smaller Palawan stink badger is unusual in having slightly paler hair underneath its body—the top and sides being dark brown to black. It has the least noticeable markings of any badger, with just a paler patch of hairs on its head and along the back.

The three species of ferret badger—the Burmese, Chinese, and Everett's ferret badgers—also inhabit southeast Asia; they are the smallest of all the badgers and the only ones habitually to climb trees. Looking like large, furry shrews they have a longer and bushier tail—half as long as the body—than their relatives and also have much richer fur coloring that is brown or, sometimes, close to red. They generally have a paler underside and striking "face mask" markings of white or yellow patches. They have the largest ears (relative to body size) of all species and their snout is long, tapering, and hairless at the tip. ■

THE BADGER'S FAMILY TREE

The nine species of badger belong to the Mustelidae family, which contains 67 species distributed almost worldwide. Other mustelids include the weasels and their allies—polecats, martens, stoats, and ferrets, the wolverine and the mink —as well as skunks and otters. Although more similar to the European badger in appearance than the ferret or stink badgers, the honey badger, or ratel, is actually only distantly related, and is classed within its own subfamily.

EUROPEAN BADGER
Meles meles (MEH-les MEH-les)

The coat color is usually a dark, grizzled gray, although gingery brown or red individuals have been found. Very occasionally, they may be pure white. The stripey facial pattern is common to these badgers right across their large range.

OTHER SPECIES
AMERICAN BADGER
HOG BADGER
TELEDU
PALAWAN STINK BADGER
FERRET BADGERS

MELINAE

HONEY BADGER

Mellivora capensis (*MELL-i-VOR-ah ca-PEN-sis*)

Only a little smaller than the European badger, the honey badger, or ratel, is distinguished by its cape of silvery-gray fur. A feature of the ratel is its skin, which is so loose that the animal can twist free of almost any grip. It is also virtually impenetrable—by teeth, porcupine quills, snakes' fangs, or bee and scorpion stingers.

ANCESTORS

POTAMOTHERIUM

Thought to be either a semiaquatic mustelid or perhaps even a very early seal, this animal is generally credited with being the earliest known mustelid. Its appearance was more that of an otter, with its long, streamlined body and flexible backbone. Its short legs ended in webbed feet with short claws. It appears to have had a fairly poor sense of smell, but probably had well developed hearing and sight: These would have been useful hunting assets as it pursued fish in freshwater lakes and rivers. Similarly, its sensitive vibrissae (whiskers) would have helped it to detect prey in silt-laden water.

Like a modern-day otter, *Potamotherium* would have been equally at home on land. Agile and sinuous, it would have coped well with the dense riverside vegetation of its habitat, leaping along with back arched and head held low.

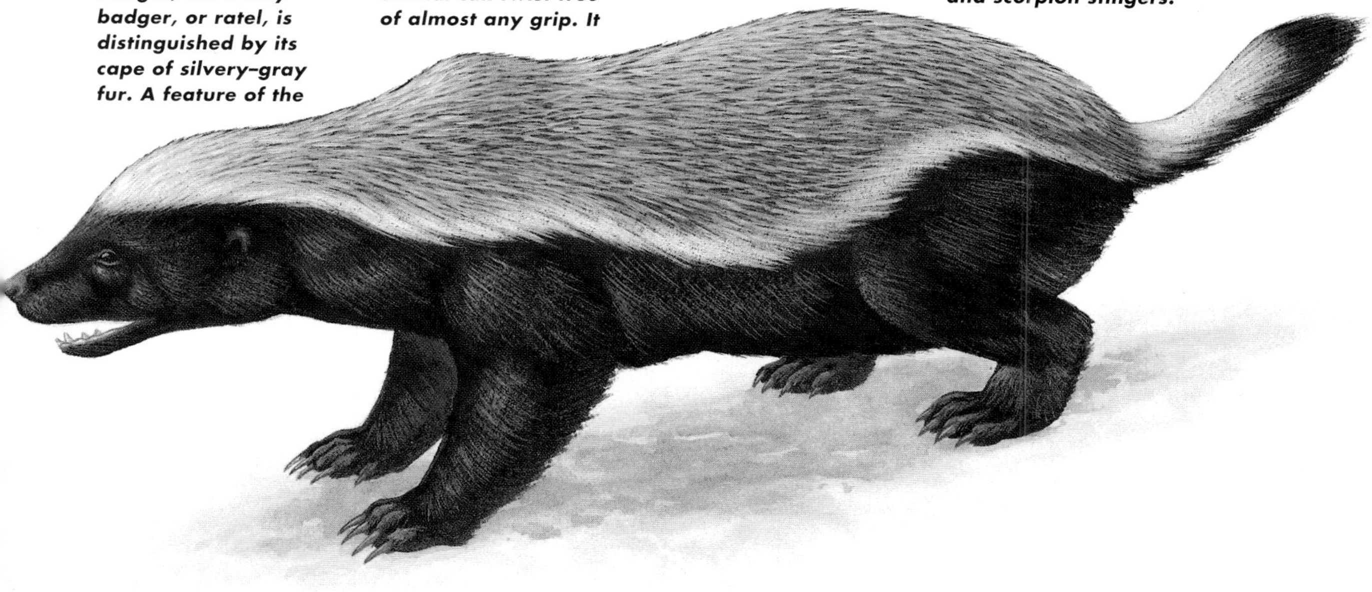

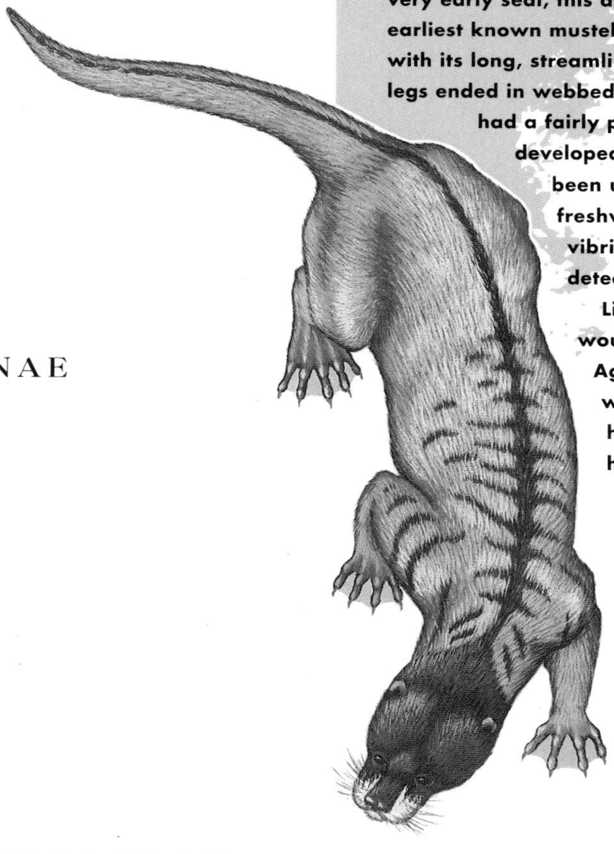

MELLIVORINAE

MUSTELIDAE

All illustrations Barry Croucher/Wildlife Art Agency

ANATOMY:
THE BADGER

hind foot   forefoot

The European badger is a squat but stocky mammal, with a maximum weight of 35 lb (16 kg). The largest of all the badgers, it is about twice the size of the ferret badgers, which, at no more than 17 in (43 cm) long, is the smallest of all the species.

THE PADS
of the feet rest on the ground, but badgers walk on their toes. There are five fixed claws on each foot. The foreclaws are longer than the hind claws.

THE JAW
gives the badger its main means of attack and defense (see SKULL). The ratel will sink its teeth into adversaries many times its size— and when a badger bites, it hangs on with relentless determination.

THE SNOUT
is long, flexible, and muscular in all badgers and is used for probing the ground to find food. Long, sensitive whiskers grow from either side of the muzzle. Sense of smell is excellent.

THE LEGS
are relatively short and are very powerful to aid digging. Badgers move with a rather rolling gait but can run very quickly in short bursts.

All illustrations Guy Troughton/Wildlife Art Agency

X RAY

THE FOOT BONES
(the metacarpals and metatarsals) are elongated and slope upward, showing how the badger actually walks on its toes.

THE SKELETON
indicates a sturdy carnivore with plenty of strong, thick bone for the adherence of powerful muscles. Although the badger's head is quite small in comparison to its sturdy body, the skull itself is actually quite large— again to provide anchorage for the massive jaw muscles.

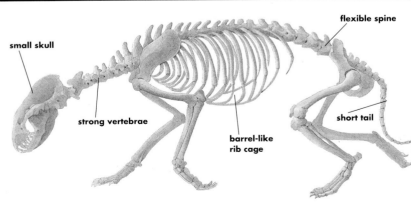

flexible spine

small skull

strong vertebrae

barrel-like rib cage

short tail

X-ray illustrations Elisabeth Smith

THE COAT

thickens in autumn. Beneath the long, coarse guard hairs lies a dense, deep underfur. The hair is thinner over the belly. The skin is thick, fatty and loose.

THE TAIL

is typically short for an animal that needs to travel fast through earthy tunnels. It does, however, vary in length relative to body size depending on species; the tree-climbing ferret badgers can claim the longest tails.

ANAL AND SUBCAUDAL

glands located under the tail secrete an oily liquid that has a strong, musky odor. It is used to scent mark territory and other badgers, as well as in defense.

...WS

...arkedly longer on ...orefeet than on the ...feet, to suit the ...er's digging and ...sive needs.

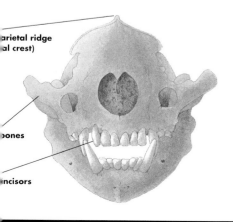

...arietal ridge
...al crest)

...bones

...incisors

THE SKULL

is about 5 in (12.7 cm) long. At ten months old the interparietal ridge arises along the crown, reaching 0.6 in (15 mm) high in mature badgers. Muscle tissue on either side of this connects with the lower jaw. The lower jaw is locked into sockets at the bases of the cheekbones. The lock is so powerful that one would have to fracture the skull to dislocate the badger's jaw.

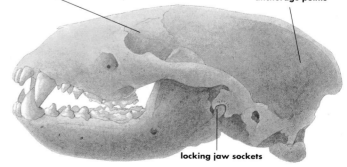

small eye sockets

deep muscle anchorage points

locking jaw sockets

WOODLAND BURROWERS

THE EUROPEAN BADGER LIVES AN ORDERED LIFE, KEEPING ITS BURROW METICULOUSLY CLEAN, GROOMING ITSELF ASSIDUOUSLY, FEEDING IN A METHODICAL WAY, AND STAYING DORMANT IN COLD WEATHER

Badgers are usually busy during hours of darkness or twilight. They spend the night foraging, often leaving the burrow, or sett, soon after dusk and returning by dawn. The American badger and the honey badger, however, may emerge during the day, particularly in the early morning or late afternoon, in areas rarely frequented by humans. Generally, a badger moves around its territory in a sort of ambling trot, its hindquarters rolling from side to side. The head is down, the large, wet nose ever active, for the badger lives in a world of scents.

FEARLESS FIGHTERS

The European badger usually avoids confrontation, but when two adults from different social groups meet—especially if one has invaded another's territory—a fight may develop. These are noisy affairs with the opponents growling, snarling, and hissing as they spin about, each trying to bite the other's rump. The badger is a tough, fearless little fighter, with its low-slung, muscled body and strong jaws that support a crushing dentition. If cornered, by a dog for example, it slashes out viciously with teeth and claws.

For aggression, the honey badger has an unrivaled reputation. It is usually silent, unless it is annoyed; then, seemingly devoid of fear, it may rush snarling from its burrow and charge directly at intruders several times its own size—horses, antelopes, and cattle have all been attacked and wounded by this ferocious little animal. The American badger, however, is among the most peaceable of all, usually backing away into its burrow in the face of a threat. If time permits, it plugs the entrance; if not, it stays at the entrance and faces its pursuer, baring its teeth and claws.

Burrowing is a feature of most badgers and many can dig amazingly rapidly. The American badger can excavate so quickly it can reputedly outpace a man with a shovel; the honey badger, too, sinks swiftly into soft ground. Badgers use this skill when building their setts, which are often elaborate and complicated structures. ∎

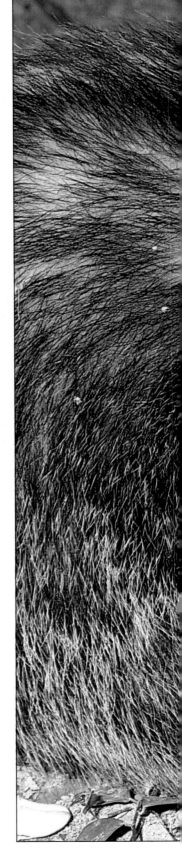

A hog badger feeding on invertebrates among leaf litter (right).

The finely tapered snout of the Chinese ferret badger (left) *is adept at seeking out prey—both on the ground and in the branches.*

Rod Williams/Bruce Coleman Ltd.

HABITATS

The European badger has by far the greatest distribution of any badger species, extending throughout Europe—with the exception of northern Scandinavia—and also throughout temperate Asia. Although primarily a woodland animal, the European badger will take to many other habitats. Besides forest, wood, and scrubland, it may dig its sett in hedgerows, embankments, quarries, moorland, and open fields, and even in natural

> BADGERS HAVE BEEN FOUND DIGGING BENEATH IRON-AGE FORTS, INTO COAL TIPS, AND EVEN IN RUBBISH DUMPS

caves or coastal cliffs. Nearby pasture and crop fields are a bonus, although badger forays into these have never been popular with farmers. The protection given by deciduous woodland, however, is the favorite, and right across its range the European badger is mainly found in such areas.

The badger usually chooses a site with well-drained soil that is easy to dig and where there is a plentiful and varied food supply close by. It sets up runways through the undergrowth that it uses regularly—these soon become well-worn routes. A need to be near water is not urgent; if the European badger has plenty of its favorite food—earthworms—it rarely needs to drink as well.

Woodlands are ideal for the badger, especially where the soil is soft (above).

The American badger (far right) is not afraid to confront a nosy coyote.

in SIGHT

THE BADGER'S STINK

All mustelids have well-developed anal glands, and badgers are no exception. When threatened, the European, American, hog, and honey badgers exude a yellowish oily fluid with a pungent, skunklike musk. The honey badger's scent is particularly vile, while the other three are mild, but it is the stink badgers that really earn their name. These small creatures can, like the skunk, squirt the liquid with deadly aim into the face of an intruder.

Although repulsive in concentrated form, these anal secretions become comparatively sweet-smelling when diluted; stink badger scent was at one time used by Javanese sultans in the manufacture of perfume.

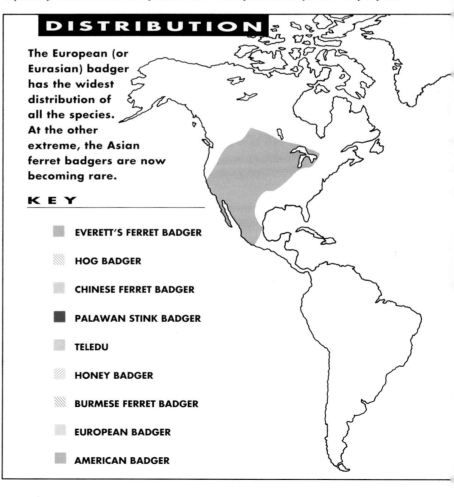

DISTRIBUTION

The European (or Eurasian) badger has the widest distribution of all the species. At the other extreme, the Asian ferret badgers are now becoming rare.

KEY

	EVERETT'S FERRET BADGER
	HOG BADGER
	CHINESE FERRET BADGER
	PALAWAN STINK BADGER
	TELEDU
	HONEY BADGER
	BURMESE FERRET BADGER
	EUROPEAN BADGER
	AMERICAN BADGER

Low-lying marshy areas are usually avoided, but, on the other hand, few European badgers live above the treeline on mountains anywhere across their range. In Britain they are found up to 1,935 ft (590 m). Woodland bordered by open pasture seems to be a particularly favored habitat. However, badgers are unlikely to choose a site that is regularly visited or intruded upon by humans.

The American badger seems more at home in open plains and farmland, only sometimes being

---

THE RATEL BURROWS LIKE OTHER BADGERS, BUT ALSO SHELTERS AMONG ROCKS AND IN HOLLOW LOGS AND TREES

---

found on the edge of woodland. It also favors relatively dry soils and countryside.

Across its range of southwestern Asia to Nepal, western India, and Africa, south of the Sahara, the honey badger may settle in most major habitats, although it is not a desert dweller. Again, it favors dry areas above others, but it is also found in forests and wet grasslands.

The hog badger is a native of the woodlands and forests of China, northeastern India, the

W. L. Miller/FLPA

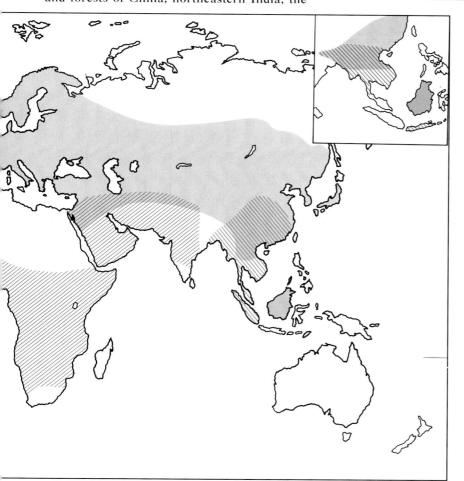

Indochinese Peninsula, and Sumatra where it may venture up to elevations of 11,500 ft (3,500 m). Again, although it digs itself a burrow, it often spends the day sleeping in such natural shelters as among rocks and crevices.

The teledu is truly a badger of the mountains, only living above 6,890 ft (2,100 m). It spends the day resting in a simple, shallow sett that is seldom

KEY FACTS

● Badgers sometimes drag sticks down into a chamber to serve as a type of mattress between the grassy bedding material and the cold, damp soil.

● An indent in a wheat field, or a hollowed space in a hedge, may be a summer nest. Badgers occasionally use these surface stopovers in places where food is abundant, then return to the sett later in the season.

● Badgers favor chalky areas, as these drain extremely well and the rocky subsoil helps to reinforce the sett tunnels. Lumps of chalk gouged with claw marks are a fairly common sight.

more than 2 ft (61 cm) deep. It may excavate this itself or it may occupy one dug by a porcupine, in which this animal may still be resident. It makes its home in the mountainous areas of Borneo, Sumatra, Java, and North Natuna Islands; on Borneo, it is said to live in natural caves. The Palawan stink badger, an inhabitant of the Calamian Islands to the northeast of Borneo, favors grassland thickets and cultivated areas.

The Chinese, Burmese, and Everett's ferret badgers, found in China, India, Nepal, Burma, and other pockets of southeast Asia, are inhabitants of wooded country—forests or bushy, tree-covered steppes—and also grassland. These smaller relatives usually dig out a simple burrow, but occasionally sleep in hollow trees or even quite high up in the crook of a branch.

TAKING TO TREES AND RIVERS

The badgers' mustelid ancestors knew how to exploit land, water, and trees—habits borne out today by relatives such as the mink and otter. However, although woodland is the commonest home of badgers, few species make much use of the available space above them; only the southeast Asian ferret badgers climb trees regularly.

FOCUS ON

EUROPEAN FORESTS

Until about 5,000 years ago, woodlands and forests of various types thrived throughout Europe. Humans have exploited woodlands ever since, so that only a small fraction of the old forests remains. Replanting schemes in this century, however, have restored some of the losses. One of France's best surviving tracts of woodland is the forest of Fontainebleau, near Paris.

Woodlands of all types are home to an abundance of wildlife. Badgers are equally at home in oak woods or beech woods, the entrance to their setts usually sited on well-drained mounds in either environment.

Woodlands comprise various layers. The topmost branches form the canopy—where the high-nesting birds are found. Beneath this is the shrub layer, where smaller trees, such as hazel and hawthorn, grow. Blackbirds, jays, and garden warblers may be found here. This layer is often thinner in beech woods, where the canopy is so thick that light cannot penetrate to allow dense growth. Beneath the shrub layer is the field or herb layer where wildflowers grow. Again, woodlands vary greatly in the amount of growth at this level. It is here, however, that the badger will be found, making its nightly forays.

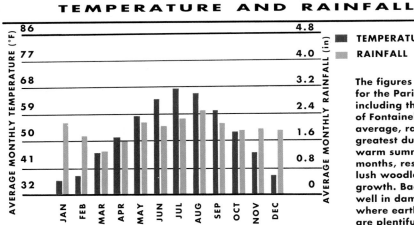

TEMPERATURE AND RAINFALL

■ TEMPERATURE
■ RAINFALL

The figures given are for the Paris area, including the forest of Fontainebleau. On average, rainfall is greatest during the warm summer months, resulting in lush woodland growth. Badgers fare well in damp areas, where earthworms are plentiful.

The honey badger is a capable climber and does so particularly in the pursuit of a bees' nest—the site of one of its favorite foods. The European badger certainly can climb if it needs to, gripping the bark of the tree with its long, curved claws in the manner of a bear. More frequently it clambers over fallen tree trunks in its path, examining them for food. It can also swim quite adequately, if it has to. The American badger seems more at home in water, swimming and even diving on hot days, and sometimes squats down in shallow water if it needs to cool down. ■

NEIGHBORS

WOOD PIGEON

TAWNY OWL

The badger shares its woodland home with a huge variety of other animals: an oak wood supports over 4,000 different species, as well as a rich diversity of plant life.

Woodlands provide a safe haven for this adaptable bird, which is also found in farming and urban areas.

This *large owl* *nests* *in tree holes. It swoops at night on mice, voles, and shrews.*

THE FOREST OF FONTAINEBLEAU

The small town of Fontainebleau is 40 miles (64 km) southeast of Paris. Some 600 years ago a royal hunting lodge occupied the site of the spectacular castle, built in the 16th century. The nearby forest is one of France's finest woodlands, covering 66 sq miles (171 sq km).

■ Melun

■ Fontainebleau

Forest of Fontainebleau

WOODPECKER

The greater spotted woodpecker sends out a staccato drumming as it picks grubs from tree bark.

YELLOW LADYBUG

Ladybugs prey voraciously on tiny flies. They fend off attackers by exuding a foul scent from their leg joints.

RED DEER

This woodland deer has a massive distribution, from Europe through to Asia and Australasia.

RED SQUIRREL

Distinguished by its rufous coat and ear tufts, this woodland mammal builds a nest high in the canopy.

RED FOX

This little hunter is often found in badger country, enjoying the deep cover and abundance of prey.

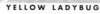

FOOD AND FEEDING

Most badgers eat whatever they can find in their habitat. The European badger is possibly the most omnivorous of all of them, and its teeth are well suited to this feeding lifestyle. It has small, chisel-like incisors and broad, flat molars that are efficient at crushing and grinding rather than chewing. The carnassial teeth—usually the teeth that help tear at prey—are inconspicuous, again more suited for grinding.

The European badger's favorite food is the earthworm, chiefly the species *Lumbricus terrestris*, which it finds in grassland and newly plowed fields in the spring. On mild, damp nights these worms emerge from their holes, and if they are in plentiful supply, the badger forages over a small area, slowly quartering the ground. By sniffing the air as it leaves the sett, the badger seems able to judge from the conditions where the best feeding grounds will be. Even when an earthworm has surfaced, it often anchors its tail end in its tunnel. But the badger keeps its nose to the ground, so it finds the worm before it has time to slip back to safety. The badger seizes the worm with its incisors, then sucks it into its mouth.

EXAMINATIONS OF THE STOMACH CONTENTS OF BADGERS SHOW THAT EARTHWORMS MAY COMPRISE FROM 25 TO ALMOST 100 PERCENT OF THEIR DIET

The badger eats windfall apples, pears and plums, raspberries, blackberries and bilberries, hazelnuts and beech mast, roots, seeds, and cereals such as corn, oats, and wheat. It snaps up slugs and snails, after first rolling them on the ground to remove the slime, as well as beetles, insects and their larvae, frogs, small mammals, and fledgling birds. The badger digs baby rabbits from their nursery tunnels and, skinning and turning them inside out, devours all but the stomach and cecum. In suburban areas, badgers rifle through garbage cans for household scraps.

Color illustrations Joanne Cowne

AMAZING FACTS

● **On a still, wet night, when earthworms are plentiful on the ground, a badger can generally find and eat about 200 in a two-hour period.**
● **Badgers will even eat carrion when they find it. A dead hedgehog, for example, offers a tasty meal; the badger carefully "peels" it to consume the contents, leaving the skin and prickles untouched.**
● **The American badger is fond of eating rattlesnakes and seems to be impervious to the venomous fangs, unless the snake sinks its fangs into the badger's nose.**
● **Honey badgers have been observed breaking through the shells of tortoises with their teeth.**

THE EUROPEAN BADGER

is a methodical feeder, quartering the ground to find every available morsel.

FOOD

As well as earthworms, the badger feeds on other invertebrates, amphibians, small mammals, nuts, fruit, and fungi. A resourceful omnivore, it adapts its diet to whatever is available in the locality of its sett.

BABY RABBIT

ACORNS

SOFT FRUITS

GREAT CRESTED NEWT

Food illustrations Ruth Grewcock

THE RATEL

Bees are a delicacy for this thick-skinned badger.

Besides rooting in the scrub with its snout and overturning clumps of soil and stones, the European badger digs shallow scrapes, up to 2 in (5 cm) deep in its search for insects. It also plows grooves along the woodland or pasture floor often up to 3 ft (1 m) long. This generally exposes a rich harvest of dung beetles—another favorite. It is partial, too, to the honeycomb, larvae, pupae, and honey from bees' nests, which it claws open, apparently impervious to the stings. Wasps' nests receive the same treatment, and it seems the badgers will often leave them alone until late summer when the wasp population is at its peak.

The American badger is probably the most carnivorous of all badgers. It preys mainly on small mammals, digging ground squirrels, pocket gophers, rats, and mice from their burrows. Above ground, it takes birds, reptiles, and invertebrates. If a badger kills a large animal, such as a rabbit, it may dig a hole and hoard it for the future. Sometimes it goes underground with its catch and stays put for a few days. Occasionally it enters a burrow that is temporarily vacant, as its occupants are hunting, and awaits their return

---

ALTHOUGH BADGERS ARE SOCIAL THEY SELDOM FORAGE TOGETHER; USUALLY THEY SPLIT UP UPON LEAVING THE SETT

The honey badger has a varied menu, but insects and their larvae, together with other invertebrates and rodents, seem to be the mainstay. It digs many of these from the ground, working with great rapidity using its forefeet and claws. This ferocious and fearless badger can kill animals as large as a small antelope. It also eats fruit and carrion, and, not surprisingly, the honey badger's name gives a clue to one of its favorite foods—not only does it eat honeybees, but the honey, too.

The hog badger's diet is similar to that of the European badger, and its long snout is particularly useful when rooting through topsoil and undergrowth. The ferret badgers are also unfussy feeders, although they seem to eat mainly animal matter and very little in the way of plants and fruits. ∎

FOOD OF THE EUROPEAN BADGER

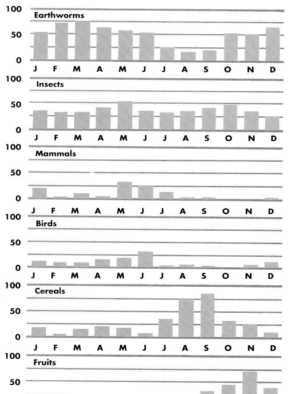

e chart to the right shows e frequency of occurrence –100 percent) of food pes through the year.

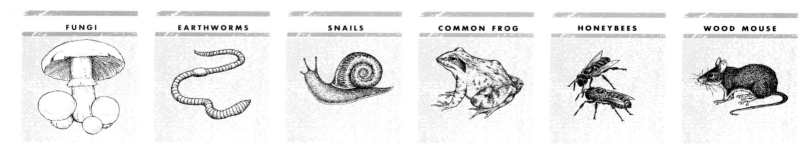

| FUNGI | EARTHWORMS | SNAILS | COMMON FROG | HONEYBEES | WOOD MOUSE |

SOCIAL STRUCTURE

The European badger is a social animal living in groups—or colonies—and occupying a home territory. Generally there are no more than 15 badgers in one group and often less. Numbers are greatest between May and September when females have cubs from that year, as well as, quite possibly, the female cubs from the previous year who may themselves have already been mated. There may be more than one adult male in a group, but there is generally one dominant boar who has prime feeding position, even pushing the dominant sow out of the way unchallenged.

LIFE IN THE SETT

The heart of a social group is the sett—an astoundingly complex burrow system consisting of many underground tunnels and chambers, generally with several entrances. Usually setts are sited within a well-drained slope, often of easily excavated, sandy or chalky soil deep within a wood. Another favored site is the border between forest and farmland. A sett may be used by successive generations of badgers, each one of which enlarges it, adding ever more tunnels—there may be as many as 90—and making mounds of earth at the entrances ever larger. Ultimately the sett can cover several acres as, after several months of living in one part of the burrow, badgers tend to tunnel to fresh areas to set up new quarters.

BADGER BEHAVIOR

When two badgers from the same clan meet during a foray, they usually scent mark each other with an anal secretion. The dominant boar in a clan generally marks other members with his scent. But if two strangers meet, they may fight fiercely, the resident animal chasing and biting the intruder, while growling loudly all the while.

As well as scent marking, badgers communicate vocally when near one another. Foraging adults give a sharp bark if another wanders too near, and frightened cubs give a high-pitched squeal.

KEY TO SETT

1 Exits
2 Latrine area
3 Nursery burrow
4 Sleeping burrow
5 Scratching tree

Illustration John Cox/Wildlife Art Agency

well-trodden paths leading away from the sett entrances, and trees near the entrances may show deep scratch marks where badgers have sharpened their claws. They also run their paws down rough trees to clean them before entering the sett.

BUSY WITH THE SPRING-CLEANING

A fastidious homemaker, the badger drags large bundles of dried plant matter underground by gathering it together between forepaws and chin, then shuffling backward down into the sett. January to May and August to October are peak times for taking bedding down into the chambers, in readiness for the winter chill. Periodically—particularly in the spring—the badger cleans out the old, musty bedding, as can be seen in the nearby spoil heap. Situated close to a sett, particularly an old one, this heap of soil, assorted vegetable matter, badger hairs, and dried feces can be enormous. On warm, sunny mornings, bedding may be dragged out just to be aired for a few hours.

Besides the main sett, a badger colony often has "outlier" setts situated within its home range. These generally have only one entrance, and usually there are well-trodden paths linking the two. These seem to be used sporadically, often by females.

Don Hunford/Planet Earth Pictures

PLAYFUL CUBS

Once given the all clear from their watchful parents, European badger cubs (above) *love to play.*

Tunnels within a burrow have been known to go 328 ft (100 m) down into the sett, but more typically they are 33–66 ft (10–20 m). The entrances to a sett are at least 8 in (20 cm) in diameter and often considerably more, with big mounds of excavated earth outside, compacted after years of being trampled upon. The burrows of rabbits—which like the same sort of ground as badgers—are marked by smaller mounds of soil and have narrower entrances. There are nearly always

A badger colony marks out a territory around its sett—the size of this varying considerably according to the type of terrain, other badgers in the area, and the availability of food. Within Britain territories have been found to vary from as small as 37 acres (15 hectares) to 3,700 acres (1,500 hectares), but an average seems to be 123–370 acres (50–150 hectares). The borders are marked by urination and defecation—usually in recognizable latrine pits. Such pits consist of several small holes about 4 in (10 cm) deep that the badger digs then uses, leaving the feces uncovered. Territories are also marked by secretions from the anal glands which the badger smears on trees and bushes. Latrine pits are also often found near a sett, although these tend to be smaller than those marking boundaries. There will also be an underground chamber for use as a latrine.

A badger habitually visits the latrine pits around the territory, often scratching furiously at the soil nearby before squatting down to pass waste matter. It generally accompanies this with a secretion from the anal glands, but badgers also "handstand" on their forelegs to rub scent on trees or fence posts in order to make their mark some 12–16 in (30–40 cm) off the ground.

FOR SHORT PERIODS OF TIME A BADGER MAY SHARE ITS BURROW WITH VOLES, WEASELS, WILD CATS, RACCOONS, AND EVEN WOLVES

The American badger apparently digs a less complex burrow; there is often only one entrance, which is elliptical in shape to accommodate this species' flatter shape. True to form, however, there is a large mound of earth by the entrance that will be compacted with droppings, bits of bone and fur, and quite often rattlesnake rattles—evidence that the American badger is partial to this venomous snake. Near the burrow there are often several other holes, similar in shape, which the badger has dug while foraging.

The honey badger is a loner, although occasionally it is seen in pairs or small family groups. Also a rapid digger, it occupies burrows, but makes its home, too, in hollow logs or trees—it is an able climber—or in sheltered spots among rocks.

HIBERNATION

Both the European and American badgers often spend days on end underground in the sett during the coldest days of winter. Yet neither is a true hibernator, for they do not enter their burrows at a certain time, and nor do they go to sleep for the

COLLECTING BEDDING

An adult gathers dry grasses for use as bedding, gripping the bundle securely between its neck and forelegs.

BRINGING IT HOME

Shuffling backward, the badger tugs the bundle down into the entrance to the sett.

OUT OF ACTION

European badgers have very few natural enemies; the greatest threat comes from humans—either through road accidents or deliberate persecution (see Survival).

The cubs of other badger species fall prey to wolves, wolverines, big cats, and owls. Some starve in dry seasons, others are killed by parents in times of threat.

Skin parasites such as lice, fleas, and ticks are a perpetual irritation—and the reason for so much grooming—but are rarely a sole cause of death.

The presence in badgers of bovine tuberculosis (TB), a cattle disease, has in the past been a cause for concern. Badgers certainly contract TB through biting each other, and may die as a result, but probably do not infect cattle. Rabies kills small numbers.

Louse

Flea

Tick

All illustrations Kim Thompson

next several months, their temperature and metabolic, heart, and respiration rate all dropping accordingly. They do, however, feed particularly vigorously in the late autumn to develop a considerable layer of fat—putting on as much as 4.5 lb (2 kg)—which will tide them through cold spells .

The most frenzied feeding, accompanied by rapid weight gain, seems to occur in October, when the European badger feeds voraciously on the autumn feast of berries. In November, it begins to leave its burrow later each night and by December, its activity has reduced considerably. Now it sleeps for much longer and much more deeply; this is also when the fertilized egg implants in the female's uterus. Well able at this time to go for long periods without feeding, a badger may

An American badger (above) taking on a rattlesnake. The snake may well end up as a meal for the mammal.

ASLEEP AT LAST

The dry grasses make a cozy bed, insulating the animal from the damp soil. The badger is a clean animal, however, and replaces the bedding regularly.

remain below ground for several days—even weeks and months at a time. During this time, it becomes torpid—that is, its temperature drops slightly and its heartbeat slows, but not to the extent of a true hibernator. Also, it will wake on warm days and emerge to forage, withdrawing again when the weather turns cold again.

Length of torpid sleep depends mainly on the climatic conditions, though badgers may still leave their burrows even in severely cold temperatures. Two American badgers were recorded staying underground for seventy consecutive days. In the northern parts of their range, European badgers may spend up to seven months underground in a torpor, while in more southerly regions, they emerge from the sett nightly all year round. ∎

LIFE CYCLE

European badgers have been known to mate at any time from February to October, yet the cubs are always born in February. This is because, in common with many other mustelids, there is a delayed implantation of the fertilized egg in the wall of the uterus. Generally, the egg is implanted in December. This delay has many benefits. It gives the adults plenty of chance to mate, the cubs are suckled when the female is still fat from her autumn feasting and is also spending the most time in the sett, and they are weaned when food is most abundant. They have plenty of time to grow and store fat for the coming winter.

Mating in badgers is a vigorous affair accompanied by a deep, throaty purring from the male and softer grunts from the female. It typically takes place at night outside the burrow, and can last for

A female European badger nursing her three-week-old cubs.

up to an hour. It is actually the act of mating that induces the female to ovulate.

Cubs are born in a specially dug chamber near an entrance to the sett to insure good air circulation. The fastidious mother fills it almost full of dry bedding to insure a cozy nest, as February can be very cold, particularly in northern climates. While the cubs are being reared, she regularly removes the bedding and replaces it anew.

There are up to five—usually two—cubs in a litter. They are born blind and tiny, weighing only 2.6–4.8 oz (75–135 g) and measuring about 5 in (13 cm). Their thin coats of silky, silvery hair have faint black stripes; it is possible to see the dark spots on their otherwise pink skin. Soon after their eyes open they begin to explore their underground home,

MUTUAL GROOMING

is important for reinforcing bonds—and a useful method of removing parasites.

YOUNG ADULTS

soon learn about the nighttime scents and sounds of the forest— what they can eat and how to find it.

THE YOUNG

may stay with their mother through the snows of winter but, come spring, she will drive them away to a new life elsewhere.

Jason Venus/Biofotos

Illustrations Evi Antoniou

GROWING UP

The life of a young badger

THESE MONTH-OLD CUBS

are just about to open their eyes. Not all cubs survive—many die during the first eight weeks, or during the few months following weaning.

WHEN CUBS FIRST EMERGE

from the sett, it is usually well after dark and they press together, keeping close contact with the mother, who constantly reassures them with a quiet purring noise.

FROM BIRTH TO DEATH

EUROPEAN BADGER

GESTATION: 8 WEEKS FROM IMPLANTATION OF EGG

LITTER SIZE: 1–5, USUALLY 2

WEIGHT AT BIRTH: 2.6–4.8 OZ (75–135 G)

EYES OPEN: 5 WEEKS

FIRST WALKING: 6–7 WEEKS

INDEPENDENCE: 14–18 MONTHS

SEXUAL MATURITY: 12–15 MONTHS

LONGEVITY IN WILD: 10 YEARS (19 YEARS RECORDED)

AMERICAN BADGER

GESTATION: 6 WEEKS FROM IMPLANTATION OF EGG

LITTER SIZE: 1–5, USUALLY 2 OR 3

WEIGHT AT BIRTH: NOT KNOWN

EYES OPEN: 4–6 WEEKS

FIRST WALKING: NOT KNOWN

INDEPENDENCE: 10–30 WEEKS

SEXUAL MATURITY: 6–12 MONTHS

LONGEVITY IN WILD: 14 YEARS

but they do not venture outside the sett until they are eight to ten weeks old.

They usually stop suckling when they are about three months old, but may feed sporadically for another month. During this time, the female regurgitates semidigested food to wean them on to solids. As the summer goes on, the cubs get bolder and indulge in lively games, although never far from the burrow. Cubs that survive often remain with the female in the same burrow all winter.

At one year old, the cubs measure about 30 in (76 cm) long with a full coat of long, thick hair. Females can mate in their first autumn, thereby giving birth when they are just one year old. Males are usually sexually mature at one year.

American badgers follow a similar pattern of reproduction to their European cousins, although

AT EIGHT MONTHS OLD, THE CUBS ARE TOUGH LITTLE ANIMALS, WELL ABLE TO STAND UP FOR THEMSELVES IF NEED BE

they tend to mate later in the year—in August or September. Two to five young are born usually in April, but sometimes as late as June in high-altitude areas. Weaned within two to three months, they leave the mother by late summer.

Honey badgers are one of the few badger species in which delayed implantation does not occur. They may mate and give birth at any time of the year, gestation lasting about six months. Commonly only two cubs are born, in a grass-lined chamber in the burrow.

Little is known about the mating habits of other badgers, although it is thought they all have delayed implantation. The true gestation in the hog badger is thought to be six weeks or less. ∎

STAUNCH SURVIVORS

MOST BADGER SPECIES HAVE SUFFERED AT THE HANDS OF HUMANS—SO MUCH SO THAT THE VERB *TO BADGER* HAS COME TO MEAN *TO BULLY* OR *ANNOY*. STILL, BADGERS HAVE SURVIVED AGAINST ALL THE ODDS

 Over the years, humans have given many reasons for killing the badger. Farmers view it as a pest—it rolls in corn, eats grain and soft fruit, digs up pastures, raids hen houses, undermines ground with its setts, and, possibly the most serious of all, seems to infect cattle with tuberculosis. In South Africa, the honey badger wreaks havoc on commercial beehives in parts of its range and is known, too, to prey on poultry, making short work of wire-netting enclosures. The American badger, ranchers claim, causes injury to cattle, horses, and people—the entrances to its burrows setting a hidden trap and resulting in broken legs.

TUBERCULOSIS SPREADS RAPIDLY THROUGH COLONIES WHEN FIGHTING BADGERS BITE EACH OTHER

To rid the land of such a pest, humans have hunted, poisoned, gassed, shot, trapped, or ensnared the badger. Few of these methods insure an instant, pain-free death and in many instances badgers have died in long and dreadful agony. Far worse than this, however, they have also been subjected to unbelievable cruelty in the so-called "sport" of badger baiting.

THE CASE FOR TUBERCULOSIS

In most cases, the damage done by European and American badgers to farmers' livelihoods is minimal: Only the occasional hen is taken—badgers cause far less carnage than a fox, for example—and losses to crops are seldom significant. Indeed, badgers are often more friend than foe, in that they destroy small rodents and rid properties of wasps' nests. In America, in particular, their burrows provide shelter for other valuable wildlife.

However, the discovery at the beginning of the 1970s that badgers contracted and passed on the disease tuberculosis (TB) to cows was viewed as very serious. Many TB-infected badgers were found, mainly in southwest England, where the badger population was not only high but where many setts were also close to cattle pastures.

Tuberculosis is contracted through breath, droppings, and urine in particular, and badgers were thought to infect cattle in various ways. As they snuffled across pastures looking for earthworms, they would contaminate the grass with their urine and saliva; latrine pits around the edges of woods or fields could be another source of infection. Badgers are also known to enter barns where cattle are kept to raid the troughs of grain. It was even thought possible that inquisitive cattle would sniff at badgers sharing the same pasture at night and inhale their infected breath.

Urban European badgers forage in a shed (right); *they are opportunists when it comes to food.*

Lee Lyon/Bruce Coleman Ltd.

A honey badger breaking into a beehive to reach the honey. It gives little heed to the bees' stings.

E. & D. Hosking/FLPA

The map below shows the European deciduous forests currently affected by acid rain.

TEMPERATE BROADLEAF

Pollution damage in the temperate forests of mainland Europe is extensive and well established. In Germany alone, the percentage of its forests that have been affected by acid rain has risen from 8 percent in 1982 to 52 percent in 1985.

Tuberculosis is known to spread quickly among badgers, as they live in such close-knit colonies. Because the incidence of tuberculosis in the southwest of England was higher than anywhere else in the country, the badgers were blamed. As a result, there was a massive attempt by the Ministry of Agriculture, Fisheries, and Food (MAFF) to stamp out the disease by destroying the badgers. From 1975 until 1982, 4,500 badger setts were gassed in this attempt.

In 1982, MAFF was informed that badgers do not die quickly when their setts are gassed; fortunately, it banned further gassing. Since that time, instead of trying to solve the problem by simply doing away with the badger population, the plan of action has been to limit the possible transmission to cattle by preventing them from sharing food sources with badgers and making sure pastures do not form badger territorial boundaries and, thus, become contaminated with latrine pits.

Today, MAFF has a special badger collection service. If you find a dead badger—either a road

John Hawkins/FLPA

Roger Tidman/FLPA

Snaring, although illegal, is still common and inflicts a long, painful death (above).

At least 45 percent of badger deaths per year (left) are caused by motor vehicles.

Badgers are willing to take food from humans and may be tempted to enter houses (below).

casualty or one that has died for any other reason—MAFF officials will come and collect it and test it for tuberculosis.

COMMERCIAL VALUE

Badgers have never really had great commercial value anywhere across their range. In some places, the European badger has been killed for its flesh, but few people develop a liking for it. In any event, as it is a host to the parasitic nematode worm *Trichinella spiralis*, eating the badger's flesh on a regular basis would be unwise. In various areas the fat has been used as a lubricant for leather goods and also to make salves and soaps, but these are of no economic importance.

Badger fur has been used for sporrans in Scotland, trimmings for hats, and for brushes—in particular shaving brushes (see page 131). In China, the European badger's pelt is apparently used to make rugs. The fur of the American badger has some value as a trim for clothes. In the 1976/77 trapping season nearly 50,000 pelts were taken in the United States and Canada, and were sold for nearly $40.00 each. However, only seven years later the value had dropped to $10.00 each, and the number of pelts taken was correspondingly less than half.

At one stage, badgers may have had some value in the pet trade. The honey badger is reported to become a meek and docile pet if captured while still young. In the United Kingdom it is an offense to keep badgers as pets unless they were obtained before January 1974. Many people do, however, put out food for them. Naturalists have mixed feelings about this. The wrong foods can cause tooth rot and food poisoning, respectively. ■

ALONGSIDE MAN

BADGERS & FORESTRY

Fences surrounding forestry can present a potential trap to badgers, particularly if they go across habitually used paths. This is something of an irony, for foresters usually welcome badgers; although they may raid a few game-bird eggs they more than make up for this by helping to control the greater threat of the rodent population.

Fortunately, in many areas, such forest fences have been modified with special badger gates. These have heavy flaps, which the badger soon learns to push against to let itself through.

Andy Rousk/NHPA

INTO THE FUTURE

Most badger species are now protected in many parts of their range, and, as we have seen, few are in any way at risk of extinction. However, besides making killing badgers illegal, conservation measures have been introduced in many places to help their continued survival.

One of the great causes of badger mortality is death on the roads—something that loss of habitat and increasing urbanization and highway systems can only make worse. In Idaho, it has been estimated that 45 percent of the American badger population is killed annually on the roads. In the United Kingdom, 1,000 badgers are killed on the roads of southwest England alone each year.

PREDICTION

BAN ON SNARES

The American Society for the Prevention of Cruelty to Animals has called for a complete ban on the use of all leg-hole traps. This would not only protect the badger but also other animals accidently entrapped.

Local authorities have addressed this problem on a number of major roads, building tunnels, and culverts expressly for badgers. It is important for these to be constructed along the routes of the animals' regularly used paths as badgers habitually use the same paths as they go out on their night-time forays. If humans choose to build a road across such a path, this will not deter the badger, for it is a creature of habit, not intellect.

Where these tunnels have been built, although suspicious at first, badgers soon learn to use the man-made structure, particularly if enticed initially with tidbits. Although such an underpass costs a significant amount of money to construct, fortunately many local authorities see it as a small price to pay to avoid serious accidents. The implications of either swerving to avoid a badger on the road or hitting an adult one with a car can be as serious to the driver and passengers as it can to the badger.

Many badgers are still caught in snares—usually set for foxes and rabbits—which can cause lingering and horrible deaths. In fact the self-locking snare is already illegal, but the use of a "free running" snare is still allowed. ■

BADGER BRUSHES

The fur of the European badger, and possibly to a lesser extent the American badger, has long been prized to make the apparently highest quality—and correspondingly expensive—shaving brushes and paintbrushes. The hairs along the animals' backs, it seems, have just the right degree of "spring and toughness" for shaving brushes. In addition, its color—white at the tip, then black, then yellowish white—became the hallmark of a quality brush.

In his book entitled *Badgers* (Whittet Books, 1988), Michael Clark estimated that a single badger pelt would probably make about ten shaving brushes and goes on to say that literally millions of shaving brushes have been made and sold over the centuries.

Since the Badger Act (1973), it is illegal to kill badgers for their pelt in the United Kingdom, and it is thought that the only place where they are still taken to make brushes is in Japan.

BADGERS IN SOUTHEAST ASIA

The ferret badgers of Indochina, Taiwan, Borneo, and outlying southeast Asian islands are the only species currently to be listed in the International Union for the Conservation of Nature's Red Data Book. They have the listing K, which means that they are suspected of being in some way threatened or endangered, but their exact status is not known for certain because of lack of information.

The stink badgers, which share some of the same range as the ferret badgers, have long been a source of food to natives, who, apparently, remove the scent gland immediately after killing the animal.

In some areas, shavings of these animals' skin are mixed with water to produce a "cure" for fever or rheumatism.

Illustration Steve Kingston

INDEX